'74 AND SUNNY

'74 AND
SUNNY

A. J. BENZA

G

GALLERY BOOKS

New York London Toronto Sydney New Delhi

G

Gallery Books
An Imprint of Simon & Schuster, Inc.
1230 Avenue of the Americas
New York, NY 10020

First Gallery Books hardcover edition July 2015

GALLERY BOOKS and colophon are registered trademarks of Simon & Schuster, Inc.

For information about special discounts for bulk purchases, please contact Simon & Schuster Special Sales at 1-866-506-1949 or business@simonandschuster.com.

The Simon & Schuster Speakers Bureau can bring authors to your live event. For more information or to book an event contact the Simon & Schuster Speakers Bureau at 1-866-248-3049 or visit our website at www.simonspeakers.com.

Interior design by Jaime Putorti

Manufactured in the United States of America

10 9 8 7 6 5 4 3 2 1

Library of Congress Cataloging-in-Publication Data is available.

ISBN 978-1-4767-3878-9
ISBN 978-1-4767-3879-6 (ebook)

At last, for Lola . . .

For bearing with me through my tears, tantrums, drinks, and dilemmas while I visited the deepest purple of my heart in writing this.

For bringing two new Benzas into this world.

For believing me when I still tell you, the best is yet to come.

'74 AND
SUNNY

1

SEASON FOR LOVING

A great day I remember was the Halloween we drove out to Jersey.

It had nothing to do with the actual drive, of course, which was monotonous in the sense that it had been done so many times before. But in taking the Throgs Neck Bridge, off Long Island, and the preferred route from my childhood home of West Islip, to my uncle Larry's house in Wharton, New Jersey, I was replaying memories from the roads I had once traveled when my father held the wheel.

Back in the 1970s, my father liked to ride all highways at what he called a "sensible speed." There was no need to put the full weight of his foot into the gas pedal as we meandered down the winding Southern State Parkway, across the magnificent bridge, and onto the mind-numbing miles of Interstates 95 and 80. And it seemed just right to him to end the drive by slowing down and coasting into the hidden lush of Route 15 and what was essentially the welcoming ramp into the front yard of my uncle's hidden home on Taylor Drive. It might've taken him an extra hour, door-to-door, but that's the way my father liked it.

But the drive I made that day, *that* Halloween, was at entirely different speeds and had a much deeper meaning. I was going to see my uncle Larry before he died.

I remember my sports car skidding on a mass of pebbles as I sharply turned into his driveway. The tray of eggplant parmigiana my mother had dutifully held on her lap the whole ride almost slid down to her feet. "Oh . . . Jesus, Mary, and Joseph!" she said.

"Oh, *they* eating over too?" I said, as I switched off the headlights and put the stick in Park. "You sure you brought enough eggplant?"

"You know what the hell I meant," she said, quickly turning somber.

My mother needed a cigarette in the dark of the car before we walked into Uncle Larry's house. "Okay, let's go do this now. Oh, Larry," she quietly exhaled. "Oh, Larry . . ." The absence of words had more meaning than anything she could've spit out. I understood the silence. Her husband—my father—had died five years earlier in 1985 and now she was essentially saying good-bye to his older brother, her loving brother-in-law and my unforgettable uncle. Two men who turned rooms upside down, who went off to the Great War when their country called, who guided each other through the first-generation experience and helped each other with the trials and tribulations of marriage and family. "Okay, your father wouldn't want us to cry," she said, as I opened the side door and pulled her out of the car by her elbows.

There wasn't much to my uncle's yard leading up to his front door. I saw a couple of strong fig trees—common in most Italian yards—bending forward in the country cold. There were several tons of large rocks and garden stones leading to a creek that sharply turned into the dark woods. And just to the left of the welcoming yellow light off his front porch, I spotted several strong peach trees that were undoubtedly pulled from my father's garden years earlier.

"Ma, look," I said, motioning to the peach trees.

She smiled. "Yeah . . . your father and his brother shared everything together."

I didn't much know what to expect upon entering the Taylor Road home. This was my uncle's second home, the one he retired to, the one he bought with his second wife, Ruth. The one his grandchildren called home. But not the one I knew best. That one was in the Succasunna.

When we stepped onto his porch, I could see his door was open a slice. I pushed it and called his name. "Uncle Larry!" I felt like our presence let loose the delicate wind chimes that were hanging above my head. "Hello . . ."

A few seconds later, I heard his voice, noticeably weaker from the raucous summers he spent with us. "That you, A.J.? Lilly?"

We crept past a few lazy calico cats that slapped at our feet while we walked.

"I'm back here in the living room," Uncle Larry yelled out. "I'm sorry I can't get up just yet. Follow my voice."

My mother shot me a quizzical look but moved on. "Don't look at me," she whispered. "I don't know what the hell to expect with your uncle Larry."

When we finally found our way around a dark staircase and we were, what sounded like, one room away, we stopped at a doorway that was adorned with dozens and dozens of twigs, and sprigs hanging from the ceiling. At first glance we might as well have been one hundred yards deep into the forest behind his house. But upon closer inspection we had stumbled on what looked and smelled like some sort of make-shift new age, woodsy medical lab.

"Is that a friggin' dream catcher?" I asked my mother.

"A *what*?" she said. "Just keep walking."

When my uncle called out to us again, he was right around the corner. "I hear you," he said. "You're getting warmer. . . ."

It felt as thick as a summer night inside Uncle Larry's living room, but when I finally laid eyes on him, he was lying on a long couch with about three layers of thick wool blankets on his chest and legs. He also had a wet washcloth stretched tight across his bald head. But you wouldn't know that his brain and lungs were riddled with cancer by the life that sprung out of his pesto-green eyes.

He made a huge effort to pull his body off the tan leather couch, but my mom and I stopped him, seeing that he was straining under the excitement and all. "Larry, Larry, stop. Don't get up. Relax," my mother said.

"Oh . . . it's so wonderful to see you both, just wonderful," he said, his eyes customarily welling up with tears. "What've you got there, Lil? Your arms are full. Is that my favorite—eggplant?"

"Of course, Larry," she said. "You know we always knock on the door with our feet."

"Oh, jeez, now I hope I have the appetite to finish all of it."

"You taught me eggplant tastes better cold the next day, on a warm piece of semolina," I said to him as he smiled and squeezed my leg.

"Larry," my mother said. "You look beat. Let me go in the kitchen and get you a glass of water or club soda or . . ."

Uncle Larry began to laugh a little. "No, Lilly. Don't worry about it. I have the chief in the kitchen working on what I need."

That sentence didn't quite sound right. My mother and I shared a look. "You have a *handkerchief* in the kitchen?" she said.

"No, no, no," Uncle Larry said, laughing through a grimace of pain coming from who knows where in his body. "I have the *chief* working in the kitchen."

That was met with blank stares.

"I guess Ruth didn't tell you," he said, sitting up on the couch and motioning us to come kiss him.

"Larry," my mother said, "I don't know who or what the hell you're talking about."

And with that, my uncle pulled the cloth from his head, straightened his robe, flashed me a giant smile and a wink, and called out to the kitchen. "Chief! Please come, come meet my brother's family."

A hulking presence of a man, wearing a flannel shirt, carpenter jeans, and work boots, walked slowly and respectfully into the room. He stood there slightly bowed, his long, thick black hair squeezed into a ponytail resting just past his shoulders. He had an expression on his angular face that suggested his being there was more than social. And in just a fleeting glance my way, I could sense he knew our drive to Jersey was rather significant.

"A.J., Lil, . . . this is my guest, Chief Lenny," Uncle Larry said. "He comes by whenever I least expect it but—it turns out—whenever I most *need* him. Right, Chief?"

The two men shared a knowing smile.

My mother was still in a little bit of shock while I extended my hand. "Chief Lenny, it's nice to meet you. I'm sure you're here for very important reasons." The chief shook my hand, smiled, and started to walk back into the kitchen. "Pleasure," he called back.

"Okay, Larry, what *is* going on?" my mother huffed. "Did you let in a trick-or-treater?"

My uncle, perhaps knowing that what he was about to tell us would be hard to digest, motioned for us to grab a seat next to him on the couch. "Let me tell you a crazy story . . ." he began. "And God help me if I'm lying."

The chief walked in the room and gave us each a cup of tea and then vanished again.

"I first ran into the chief—or I should say the chief ran into *me*—when the headaches started," my uncle began. "Not just headaches, mind you, but headaches so bad that I felt blinded by even the smallest of light entering a room. Not even the light of a firefly passing the window could sneak by without the migraines getting worse."

My mother told him she remembered he wasn't even taking calls when the debilitating headaches began about a year earlier.

"This is well after I had gone through the initial chemo and radiation on my lung. And right before I was to be diagnosed on the spots on my brain," he said, motioning for us to sip our teas. "It's very hard being a doctor with cancer, because we in the profession are the first to place odds on a patient. I knew mine were very, very low."

"But you and my father are fighters, Uncle Larry, and fighters always have a puncher's chance," I said. He put his hand up rather weakly. "Perhaps that's true, A.J. But cancer is never the underdog in a fight. It enters the ring, it comes into your body, as the favorite."

"So . . . the chief," my mother interrupted. "How'd you meet the chief?"

"I'm sorry. My mind wanders," he said. "It was a rainy night, I want to say about a year ago. Once again, I'm on this couch suffering a headache so bad even the raindrops on the roof hurt."

"Oh, Larry . . ." my mother whispered.

"On top of the headaches I had developed a lousy cough earlier in the week. So I was really suffering. Suddenly I hear some tapping on the back sliding door, and I'm thinking it's some opossums or rabbits or some other *creatura* out there in the woods that want to be fed."

"Or maybe those black bears are back from a few years ago," I offer.

"At this house, who knows," he said.

My uncle took on almost a reverential tone when he went on with the next part of his story. A story that wouldn't have been so damn believable if it hadn't been staring us right in the face the whole time we were there.

"I used every last bit of strength I had to rise off the couch and shuffle to the door and peer through the raindrops on the glass. And godammit if it wasn't an Indian staring right back at me," he whispered. "A fuckin' Indian with feathers in his long hair and paint on his face. Standing right there on my deck, on a rainy night in Jersey. If that don't beat all."

It still didn't connect with my mother. "You were seeing things!"

"No, Ma," I said. "Uncle Larry's saying that Indian was the chief."

Uncle Larry laughed and shook his head in unison with mine.

"The chief has saved me, Lilly. He's kept me around a lot longer than modern medicine could."

My mother was incredulous. "Larry, why didn't you tell any of us about this?"

"Would anybody have believed me if I had said an Indian drops by sometimes to help me live?"

"So, is he a witch doctor or what?" my mother asked.

"He's not a witch doctor. He's Chippewa nation, from an organization known as Midewiwin."

As my uncle Larry laughed at the expression of shock on my mother's face, the chief's lumbering footsteps came from the kitchen and joined us by the couch before he handed my uncle a cup of something.

"What's this I'm drinking, Chief?" Uncle Larry asked, before motioning for his friend to shed more light on his being there.

"Of course, Doctor," the chief said. "This is just a little wild onion and wild garlic tea, with a small hint of mountain sweet. To help with your breathing and to beat back those small tumors. Also to encourage probiotics."

"Well, I'll be damned," I said.

The chief turned his attention to my mother. "We in

Chippewa nation use material remedies that are the secrets of our organization. We believe that every tree, bush, and plant has a specific use. And that is the knowledge I bring to brother Larry."

Uncle Larry sipped from his cup. "But, best of all, I never had to tell Chief here I was sick. He came to me that rainy night because he sensed the spirit of suffering lay in this house. Ain't that right, Chief?" Uncle Larry said.

"How the hell do you do that?" I said.

"Yes, Doctor," the Chief said as he pointed to his head and chest. "Your uncle's pain directed me here. It did not matter that we were strangers. What mattered is that we were destined to meet."

As my mother sat down in a heap, blown away by the fairy tale of it all, Uncle Larry told the chief to walk me around the kitchen to take a look at all his medicines and potions. "Give him the tour," he said.

The chief walked me into the kitchen, where he had taken over a whole wall and countertop for all his wares. There were dozens and dozens of leaves tied into packets and twigs tied into bundles. My father taught me enough about nature for me to see remnants of spruce sprigs and leaves belonging to hemlock and creeping snowberry plants. I even pointed out, to the chief's delight, a bunch of red raspberry and portulaca.

"You were taught well," the chief said to me, tapping my shoulder. "Let me show you a little of how we use nature's bounty."

He told me that on that first night, he wandered through the woods—he and my uncle's pain his only compass—until he came upon the back porch of a home set back from Taylor Road. He brought with him a large leather pouch filled with the remedies he sensed he would need. "The inner scrapings of bur oak to immediately help the doctor's heart and circulatory system as well as Labrador leaves and root of dogbane for the severe headaches and affliction of nerves."

After a seventy-two-hour marathon of administering these remedies—in which the chief never slept a wink—he knocked my uncle's pain clear out of his body. More important, it slowed his cancer to a crawl. This feat allowed the chief to ease my uncle past the world of just sipping on teas stirred with a stick.

"What other stuff did you use?" I said, running my fingers across numerous bottles of powders and elixirs, like wintergreen, joe-pye weed, boneset, and pennyroyal. "After the initial visit, your uncle was game for anything," he said. "And I got to work. And I didn't stop until we felt better.

The chief told me he would scrape the inner bark of dried bur oak mixed with dogbane root and pulverize it enough so that it could be snorted as a powder. Or he would gather up and mix spruce sprigs, hemlock leaves, chokecherry, and wild cherry twigs and pound them into a powder and place them on hot rocks so my uncle could cover up under a wet towel and inhale the strong and healing fumes. Other times he would pulverize dried yarrow leaves and combine them with mild tobacco, bearberry, and red-willow leaves to be smoked in a pipe.

"It was most important that I got bobea, wild snowball, and mountain sweet into the doctor's system first," the chief said. "I felt the pain leave us from our lungs first and next the very blood running throughout our bodies."

"Mom, you have no idea how cool all this is," I shouted into the other room.

The chief laughed. "Usually I mix a tea with root bark and goldenseal each night before bed for your uncle," he said. "But I don't think he will need it tonight."

"What's that tea for?"

"Despondency and melancholy." He smiled. "I know he feels happy that you are here, because I feel happy that you are here."

I thanked the chief for all he told me about helping my uncle by shaking his hand and hugging him hard around his back. It seemed out of place and very ordinary for all the mystical and otherworldly stuff he had just shared with me. When I walked back into the den, it was obvious from their expressions that Uncle Larry had shared some special things with my mom, perhaps more accurate things, concerning his health.

My uncle called out to me. "I was just telling your mother, A.J., how much that summer of 1974 meant to me and your aunt Geneva."

"Summer of '74," I said. "Yeah, that was a great movie."

"Don't be a smart-ass," my mother snapped. "That was the summer we watched Gino for a few months while Aunt Geneva recuperated from her surgery."

"I know, I know. I'm just breaking balls," I said. "Yeah, that was one helluva summer I had with my little cousin tailing me. I know I'll never forget it."

"My family was just here the other day talking about it," Uncle Larry recalled. "All the girls and their kids. Robin, Susan, Geneva, it was just wonderful. Gino and Glen were here too. So happy, my son is. So handsome! I don't know why I ever worried."

"Spitting image of his old man," I said.

"But you'll never know how much that summer meant to me as a man," Uncle Larry knowingly said to me. "One day, you'll be a father yourself. And you'll never expect that there'll come a day when it's not enough to be the *only* man in your little boy's life."

His eyes were welling up a little, so I tried to shake us back to reality. "Ah, come on, Uncle Larry. Ain't there a tea Chief, here, can make to get us to quit getting so sad?"

But my uncle Larry would rather live in the moment, however uncomfortably beautiful it was. "Look at me," he said, running his hand down his torso. "I used to hold my health in an iron fist and say things like, 'That's not what I imagined would happen to me.' Well, the grip has loosened now, so I can let it just be what it is."

I looked over at my mother, who was working a tissue

like she knew she wouldn't be seeing her brother-in-law too much longer. "I told Uncle Larry how it sometimes bothers you that we signed a paper for the doctors not to resuscitate your father," she said. "He wants to say something to you."

"Ah, Ma, not that again . . ."

"No, no, no. Listen to me, A.J.," Uncle Larry said with a soft smile. "He's not up there upset that you guys did what you did. He was *counting* on it. My brother and I talked. And I hope my son does the same thing if it comes to that."

"Now you're talking crazy, Uncle Larry."

"No, A.J. You know what's crazy? Crazy is an Indian chief in your kitchen."

2

TAKIN' CARE OF BUSINESS

I thought of my father as old all my life. Not the type of old that would indicate any kind of fragility. The type of old that suggested a lack of patience for things that used to come so easily, like throwing a spiral to his only son, or getting out of his favorite recliner without a boost. The type of old that simmered with the exasperation at the changing of the times, at the world around him and the people who were taking it over. An old that bubbled with anger at the suggestion that his way may no longer be the best way. That his opinion, despite his wisdom and worldliness, no longer held water.

Not that he ever shied away from making his opinion known. One morning I watched as my father, shirtless, bent over to bury his head deep into the refrigerator (or icebox as he called it), muttering to himself in Sicilian. After a few minutes, he popped his head out and called to my Neapolitan mother, a saint of a woman who always knew how to toss a wet blanket onto his fiery spirit.

"Lilly, do me a fuckin' favor, would ya? Don't buy the *tub* of Breakstone's Butter no more. Every fuckin' time I open it up to spread some on a piece of semolina, I gotta see all the crumbs from whoever the hell used it before me."

"All right, all right," my mother said, dropping whatever she was doing to make it all better. "I'm sorry, Al. There was a sale."

"It's just a thing with me, Lilly. Just don't do it. Is that so hard?"

"No, no, you're right. I'm not even that crazy about it. I'll throw it out."

Of course, that wasn't really what was eating at him at the time. The butter fight was his outlet for whatever was really on his mind.

My older sisters and I, sitting in front of the TV, knew what was to follow. After all, this was 1974. The president was in disgrace, and young GIs were suffering in the jungles of Vietnam; gas lines stretched out for miles, New York City was going to shit, and I was struggling with pimples and puberty in a tough-love Sicilian-American household. On top of that, Archie Bunker was dealing with a black neighbor. Maude had had an abortion. And Mary Tyler Moore was going to "make it after all." All this stuff was happening too quickly for my father, Al Benza.

"I'm gonna tell you all something before I go to work. The *TV Guide* says *West Side Story* is on the television tonight." He was just getting started. "If I come home and find out any of you watched it, I'm gonna put my foot through the screen and no more TV. *Capiche*?"

My middle sister, Lorraine, who was wild for Richard Beymer, spoke up.

"Oh, Daddy . . . why? I love *West Side Story*. Why do you hate it?"

Now he was in the zone. "Because it promotes Puerto Rican gang violence and I'm not gonna have that in this house. It's enough these spics have invaded New York City with their fuckin' switchblades and cockroach-killer shoes. I don't wanna see it in my house."

My sister Rosalie, who was twenty-nine, married and lived with her husband Jack and their two-year old son, Jackie, in the house next door, was the only one with the balls to ask the real question. Maybe because Jack was half Puerto Rican.

"But why is it okay that we went to see *The Godfather* twice in the same week at the movies? That was more violent than *West Side Story*, and—"

He cut her off and bent down to look her in the face. The black eyes they shared were inches apart.

"Listen to your father. *The Godfather* is about *family*, *love*, and *honor*," he said through clenched teeth. "The other one is horseshit. And you know how much I love Jack."

"All right, Al, all right," my mother said. "Don't drive to work mad. The kids won't watch the movie."

Of course, later that night we all watched *West Side Story* until we heard his red convertible Mustang glide into the driveway.

On some school mornings, I remember using the ridiculously massive lion's head brass door knocker my father had mounted above the knob to their master bedroom. I would come into the smoke-hazed room to a fully naked father shaving in the mirror and my mother in a worn-out muumuu. I often needed ten cents for lunch money. When things were really tight financially my mother used to silently open the top drawer to my father's magical dresser—the one with the pistols, the lock picks, and the naked-lady playing cards—and fish out a "wheat" dime from my father's prized-but-pitiful coin collection. "Don't tell your father," she'd warn me. I also remember how some teachers, upon seeing the older, out-of-circulation dime, would swiftly pocket it and switch it out with one of their newer-minted coins.

My father got dressed for work and came downstairs smelling of Winston cigarettes, Old Spice cologne, and Dentyne chewing gum, calling, "Now all you *sombitches* come give *yo* poppa a kiss." He kissed my mother, then pinched her on the breast and gave her a hard smack on the ass.

"That hurt. You bastard."

"I love you too. Go fuck yourself."

It went like that between my mother and father.

. . .

The year I turned twelve, it became somewhat of a customary job for me to pour my father a tumbler of Scotch the minute he walked in after a fourteen-hour workday. He was never particular about the Scotch he drank. In fact, he often dared anyone to tell the difference between a shot of Johnnie Walker and a bottom-shelf brand, the kind that usually came with a handle on the bottle. I had gotten used to letting my top lip touch the whiskey before I handed him his glass, but he'd often see me shudder as I handed him his poison.

"You'll get used to it," he'd say. "But don't ever drink it without me knowing about it. Promise your father."

"I promise, Daddy. It burns my mouth anyhow."

"Wanna know the best thing about Scotch? Never gives you a hangover. Thirty years I'm drinking Scotch, never had a hangover, woke up sick, nothing."

"That's a helluva great thing to tell your son, Al," my mother would say.

"Who's gonna tell him when I'm dead? *Thirty years*." He'd wink at me, and I'd watch him down his first glass and ask for a second. That was the one he'd take into the kitchen and enjoy with his ten o'clock supper, as my mother and I sat next to him and listened to him tell us his tales of the day as a carpet and linoleum salesman for Kaufman Carpet.

Most of the stories were peppered with references to his superiors as kikes or *mazo Christos* (Christ killers), and to some of the customers as cocksuckers or schmucks because they couldn't make up their minds and denied him a sale. My mother would listen intently, letting the volcano bubble a little, but always pacifying him before the lava started to roll down the mountain. And I would sit there at the table and tell him about my day.

One night he came in with a glint in his eye. He handed me a gallon of bottom-shelf Scotch he'd bought and told me to take it to the bar in the TV room.

"Where's Fat Ro?" he asked, his inside joke for Rosalie's near-perfect figure. "Where's my NuNu?" That was his nickname for Lorraine. "Everyone asleep but you and your mother?"

"Yep."

"Well, that's too bad."

I knew he could tell something was wrong.

"School was good today?" he asked.

"Yeah, you know, it was all right."

"Well," he said between bites. "School is school. If it were fun, they'd call it 'play.'"

"Yeah, I guess."

"What'd they teach you today?"

I had to be careful. That day's school lesson was about immigration. And, to my father, the only immigrants who mattered were Italians. The rest were quickly dismissed or easily characterized: The Irish were drunks. Moolies were no good. Jews were cheap bastards. Germans were as cold as ice. Polish were stupid. Hispanics were lazy. The French were fags who couldn't fight.

"The teacher was telling us about what the Statue of Liberty means to people from other countries," I said. "She was saying that it is just as special for immigrants today as it was for people who came over in the 1900s."

"You know your grandparents came over from Italy on those ships?"

"I know," I said.

"And the Whore in the Harbor is the last sight I can remember seeing when I got on that ship that took me overseas to fight in World War Two. She's a very special thing."

"Why do you call her that?" I asked. "The Whore in the Harbor."

He threw back his last gulp of Scotch. "Because with the amount of nationalities we got coming here now, she might as well have one leg raised over her head."

I chuckled a little.

"Come on," he said. "That was funny. What happened? You're not telling your father everything. Who bothered you today?"

My mother rolled her eyes and bit down on the knuckle of her index finger, as if begging me not to bring up anything that wasn't going to wash down smooth with his arduous day and his double Scotches.

"Well . . ." I stammered, as my eyes brimmed with emotion. "We were picking sides for tackle football in the school yard and Jimmy Piga told me I couldn't play."

"Who's this Jimmy Piga?"

"He's, like, a tough kid. He's a year older. Some of the guys say his father is in the Mafia."

My father dropped his utensils and pushed his dish away. He turned to my mother, who was busying herself at the stove or the refrigerator, as far away as she could get from the volcano.

"Lilly, I want you to come over here and listen to me," he said. "I'm seeing bloodred right now. I can't eat."

He wiped the corners of his mouth with his *mopina* (kitchen towel), folded it lengthwise, and snapped it violently over his shoulder. Then he pushed back in the kitchen chair, so he was leaning against the wall with the chair balancing on its rear legs. He spoke with the precision of a surgeon in the OR.

"Here's what you're gonna do. I want you to put a brick in your book bag. And you take it with you to school tomorrow. And when this Jimmy Piga says you can't play again, I want you to take out the brick and break it over his fuckin' skull."

I was confused but knew I had to nail every detail of his plan to show I fully comprehended his revenge plot. "You mean . . . just throw it at him?"

"No. Listen to me. Take the brick and break it over his head. And if he has a problem with that, you tell him to bring his fuckin' father over here and I'll deal with him. Either you deal with this Piga kid, or you deal with me tomorrow. You understand? I love you too much to have some prick treat you that way. You're a Benza. You don't take shit from no one. Now gimme a kiss and hit the rack."

"Dad . . . it's not that big a deal . . ."

"Nah, nah, nah," he said, smoothing out the tablecloth. "Whenever someone is doing you *wrong*, you gotta have the balls to make it *right*."

"Okay, Dad."

"Come here . . . have a taste of your mother's caponata."

"No way," I protested. My mother's caponata was a dish made from the discards of every vegetable in the house, sautéed with olive oil and fresh garlic from our garden.

"It's ABC delicious," he said. "Okay, whatever you wish. More for me, then."

I felt guilty leaving my mother behind to deal with his anger. But I kissed them good night and went to bed, all the while envisioning how I was going to break a brick over Jimmy Piga's head. Or how I would have to deal with my father if I didn't. My father had never laid a hand on me in my life, but just disappointing him would have crushed my world.

I started up the steps and I side-eyed my father motioning to my mother with his fork. "What'd I say? Am I wrong?"

"No, Al." My mother sighed. "What am I gonna tell you?"

The next day, when it came time to choose sides for tackle football—or Rumbles, as we called it—and Jimmy Piga once again told me I couldn't play, I followed my father's instructions to the letter. I walked away from the game, sat down by the flagpole, and fished out the red brick from my book bag. And while Piga was scribbling a play in the dirt with his index finger and some small twigs, I calmly walked to the huddle and cracked the brick over the back of his head. By the time it rolled down his back and settled at his feet, I felt a quick rush of adrenaline telling me to grab it again and hold it above my head.

"What the fuck, are you crazy?" he stammered, while falling to his side. "He just hit me on the head with a brick," he told a dozen frozen friends. "My fuckin' ears are ringing!"

"I'm playing in this game, Piga," I said, with the red brick firmly in my right hand. "I'm playing every day. If you don't like it, my father said to tell your father to go see him. And he'll bust his skull wide-open."

Jimmy Piga, whose red eyes bulged with confusion and stymied anger, never told his father. And I never missed a game of Rumbles ever again.

When I told my father what had happened, the next night over one of his late dinners, he lit up like a firefly.

"You see what I told you? See what I told you? That's great. That is so great! This is the way you settle matters. We gotta have the good Scotch tonight."

He leaned over and kissed me hard on the mouth. I didn't even mind that his lips tasted of pasta con *sarde*—sardines.

. . .

Although I was only a kid, I was deeply dug into the front lines of the war my father was fighting with the world around him. His foes included everything from ageism to organized religion, feminism, dope in the school yard, the social politics of Pop Warner football, alcoholism, the anticipated journey of his golden years, and a curious and painful skin condition that had every dermatologist within a fifty-mile radius completely baffled. It was a war fought on too many fronts and against too many inexhaustible enemies. But as the loyal son of Alfredo Benza (and, as fate had it, the last Benza boy to carry on his Sicilian bloodline), I fought alongside him. And when I wasn't fighting, I sat at his feet and absorbed everything he had to say.

My father was the last of a dying breed, a man who stayed true to the very essence of himself. He gave me an appetite for truth and the desire to do something worthwhile, so that one day I'd have as many stories told about me as the million or so everyone told about him. Like the movie star legends he urged me to watch when he wasn't around—Garfield, Mitchum, Cagney, or McQueen—I wanted to stand up for myself, stand up for something, even if it didn't end happily.

"People are going to ask you to eat shit," he would say. "Just don't develop a taste for it."

He never said as much out loud, but I believe my father was hell-bent on making sure I could navigate my way toward manhood, even without his being around very often. He was a salesman in his fifties, with too many younger men getting too close for comfort when it came time to make commissions. He would often scoff at the thought of a day off, and too many times I can remember him working seven days a week. Or maybe it was on account of the sea of women he left me with every day as he went off to work. Of course, there was my saint of a mother, who worked as a lunch lady at my elementary school across the street—complete with the horrifying hairnet and the white rubber-soled shoes worn by cafeteria employees and Nurse Ratched. And when school was out, I got to run home across the street to see my aunt Mary, my father's eldest sister—who never married but traveled to Hawaii *thirty-one times* over the years to visit her "friend" and hula instructor, Emilani. Whenever Aunt Mary wasn't playing Don Ho records, she was usually sunning her sixty-four-year-old body in a leopard-print two-piece on the deck of our aboveground redwood pool. And Aunt Mary, God rest her soul, was no Helen Mirren. That made having friends over a mortifying experience.

Sure, my father had a great *Playboy* collection lying around, but listening to "Tiny Bubbles" or watching Aunt Mary slowly swim laps destroyed the mood for any one-handed alone time I was actively trying to carve out for my then obsession, Miss May 1974, Marilyn Lange. It would take months to seal that deal.

My father's sister-in-law Mae (recently widowed from

his brother Philly) and my hot sixteen-year-old cousin, Arlene, lived two houses away and came over every chance they got. Aunt Mae to gossip over Entenmann's crumb cake, and Arlene to hang out in my sister Lorraine's room and listen to 45s of Chicago, the Guess Who, Donovan, and the like. Sometimes they would read passages from a hidden copy of *Our Bodies, Ourselves*, write imaginary love letters to Jimi Hendrix, make collages of Twiggy's magazine layouts, and sneak drags of Eve cigarettes by the open screened window. Sometimes they would play Carole King's *Tapestry* so loud, I would army-crawl into her room—my face practically tasting the shag rug—and listen to them talk about stuff like hickeys and periods and discharge. When those conversations started, I would stand up like a shot—scaring the shit out of both of them—and interrogate them like a prosecuting attorney until they disclosed what each term meant. And, little by little, they would tell me. Learning about hickeys and menstrual cycles was priceless, but they stood firm at discharge. Somehow they knew that was crossing the line for a twelve-year-old smart-ass. They got all serious on me and spoke in hushed tones before finally assuring me that the "discharge" they were referring to only meant my cousin Ray—Arlene's brother—was getting sent home from Vietnam on account of Uncle Philly dropping dead after his fifth heart attack.

"We said discharge because he was *discharged* from the army!"

Deep down I knew it meant something else, but I let it go.

Our house really came to life when my sister Rosalie would bolt through the kitchen screen door and surprise everyone with what was usually an unbelievable story after her shift ended as a teller at the Bank of Babylon. If she wasn't finding and caring for a box of abandoned kittens or cursing my father for sneaking his .38 caliber handgun in her pocketbook while she was at the bank, then it was usually a story involving her infamous battles on supermarket checkout lines. My sister never started a fight, but she finished them all.

"I'm at King Kullen tonight, and this woman behind me, I can see, is counting my items because I'm on the express line. Ten or less. I had eleven because I forgot I needed a chunk of provolone for Sunday." Rosalie is saying this, out of breath and holding a rescued kitten in each hand. "Under her friggin' breath, I hear this woman say, 'Go ahead, let the guinea get her cheese.'"

Gasps all around the table.

"What did you do?"

"Please don't tell your father."

"Can I go back to the store without being embarrassed?"

Rosalie went on. "Well, I turned around and I grabbed her head with both hands and I said, 'Who. The. Fuck. Are. You. Calling. A. Guinea, you Irish bastard?' Just like that. And the cashier is screaming, 'Please girls, stop.' But it's too late. The manager comes over all worried, saying, 'Ladies, what's going on? What's the problem?' I say, 'Nothing.' The Irish girl can't even talk, she's so shocked. And . . . I walk out with my eleven items."

"Oh, Rosalie . . ." my mother tried.

"Ma, I gotta hear her call me a guinea? Since when?"

"Oh, Christ, they're all like their father, except my Lorraine," my mother said.

I always managed to run to the table and hear the tail end of my sister's battles. "Why doesn't this happen when you go shopping with me? I wanna fight someone at King Kullen," I'd say.

"I'm not even going to tell your father, because he'll go to the supermarket and wait for the manager to come out and there'll be a real shit storm," my mother would say. "This is between us. Don't tell your father!"

"That's not even why I'm here," Ro said. "Get Lorraine and Arlene. I wanna put Tiger Lilly in a doll's dress and find a little black top hat for Lorenzo [our cats] and film a wedding ceremony tonight."

Before you knew it, we were digging through bags in the garage and retrieving tiny doll clothes for the cats to wear for their shotgun wedding—all caught on our Super 8 mm camera. Within an hour of Rosalie's dropping in, we were all planning a ridiculous feline wedding, and that clip still exists to this day—almost forty years later. And it gets the same laughter time and again. That's one of the reasons why you had to be around the magical aura of my sister Rosalie whenever she walked into a room. You had to turn your chair in her direction. She made you look.

When the house finally turned quiet, when Rosalie took her show home, Aunt Mary dozed off on the downstairs couch in front of the TV that I would secretly turn to the X-rated Escapade channel), Aunt Mae and Arlene walked home, and Lorraine fell fast asleep within minutes of her lights turning off, that was usually when I'd be under my covers and hear the ice clinking in the tumbler of my father's third Scotch. That was the one he took past my bedroom and brought into his own before collapsing into his king-size bed. I'd listen to my mom carefully pleading with him to calm his anger when he'd discuss the corporate bosses or loopy customers who dropped by the store with stupid requests or silly demands. I could hear her undressing him and dropping his head on the pillow.

"Oh, Manoola." That was the nickname he gave her. Nobody knew why. "I wish you could see the shit I have to go through every day with these crooked kikes. They all have mistresses, and they would sell their own mothers down the river to turn a dollar profit."

"All right, Al, I know. It won't always be this way," my mom would promise him as he passed out. He would begin snoring immediately, and she would finally be able to light a cigarette and pop a Librium to adjust her high blood pressure and calm her down.

Sometimes she would walk into my room and sit on my bed, smiling and laughing nervously to reassure me. "Oh boy!

Well, your father was in rare form tonight," she'd say, whistling through her teeth and rubbing my chest. "He was feeling a little bit stewed. Don't worry, honey. If you hear him yelling, always remember Daddy's under a lot of pressure at work. He works hard for us."

"I know, Ma. I know what Daddy goes through," I'd whisper, closing my eyes. "I listen."

The call that changed my life that summer was, while unexpected, not out of the ordinary. For reasons unknown to me, our family's upstairs telephone line was not in my parents' master bedroom. Instead, the big, white rotary machine sat on a tiny glass-topped, wrought-iron stand right outside my bedroom, down the hall from my parents' door. This unfortunate placement gave me horrifying access to the sudden and sometimes gory details of the deaths of almost all my aunts, uncles, cousins, and some really close acquaintances. By the time I was four years old, I had already lost both sets of grandparents. By the time I was twelve, I had grown accustomed to the phone ringing at ungodly hours, hearing my mother trying to slip on her Dearfoam slippers as she raced down the hall and stopped at my door to receive what was undoubtedly a death call. Maybe there are some families out there who wait for the breakfast hour, at least, before delivering the bad news. My family delivered it as it came, even at two in the morning.

It usually took my mother five or six rings to even get to the phone, but when she did, I would already be wide-awake and sitting up in my NFL sheets, staring at the posters of Farrah Fawcett and the Fonz on the opposite wall.

"Josie died! Oh, Al, my sister Josie died," my mother would yell down the hall. "Ahhh . . . poor thing. She suffered enough. At least she's out of pain now."

Or:

"Millie's dead? When? How?" And then the details would be relayed to my father right outside my door. "She was throwing up blood for two days. Her lungs were just shot. They had tubes in her throat and in her side trying to clear her chest, but she went tonight. Ah, shit, and now my brother Louie has chest pains and a numb left arm! Jesus Christ, Louie, have them check you out. You're *there now*!"

And:

"Yeah, Mae! What's wrong? Eileen was killed in a car accident? Oh my God! Thirty years old. Somebody ran a light on Sunrise Highway and plowed right into her. She died in Gregory's arms. Oh, Mae . . . what can we do?"

Calls like those would prompt my father to wake up the entire family, sober up immediately, and invite the grief-stricken family over for coffee and his famous *verdura* omelets. It wasn't unusual for relatives of ours to drive from Brooklyn to our home in West Islip, Long Island, some fifty miles away, and go over the funeral and wake details right at our kitchen table.

On those days, my father would forbid me to go to school. He wanted me to see the grief and be there to lift the spirits of my cousins whenever I could.

"Listen to your father," he'd say to me, kneeling down. "This is more important than anything you're gonna learn in school today. You be here for your family."

This particular late-night phone call, however, the one that changed my life that summer, made me sit up in bed and pay closer attention, because this time no one had died or was facing a terrible illness. This call had a different tone. My mother passed the phone to my father almost as soon as she picked up. It was dead quiet in the hallway, and that meant I could hear every syllable that was coming out of the receiver, as well as my father's calming words.

It was the sobbing voice of my father's older brother, Larry. Uncle Larry was a doctor who lived in New Jersey and had a very successful medical practice. Through the years, Uncle Larry had been there for us many times when my father's salary was not enough; he'd graciously send a check along to make sure our monthly nut was covered. He had three daughters, Geneva, Susan, and Robin, and two sons, Larry Jr. and ten-year-old Gino. By the time the summer of 1974 came and went, it was no surprise—but a hell of a shock to my macho uncle Larry—that his oldest son, Larry, was looking forward to leaving home and starting a somewhat mysterious new life in San Francisco.

Although he was a well-respected doctor, Uncle Larry couldn't bring himself to refer to his son as a homosexual. He, along with a lot of other professionals, preferred the term "brain damaged."

A. J. BENZA

So when the phone rang outside my door that summer night in June 1974, I heard my uncle coming to grips with the fact that his youngest boy, Gino, was going the way of his older brother.

I cracked my door open a slit to see the action.

"Al," said Uncle Larry. "I'm fucked. I'm fucked, I'm afraid, and I don't know how to handle this. I'm afraid my Gino is brain damaged too. I don't know what to do, Al. I don't know what to do."

If it weren't so sad, it would have had all the high drama of Johnny Fontane crying to Vito Corleone.

"What the fuck are the odds? How do you know?"

"Alfred. A father just . . . knows."

I heard Uncle Larry stop to light a cigarette, exhale the smoke, and take a swig from a glass of whiskey. The clink of the ice cubes, sounded like three of them, came across the wire crystal clear.

My father covered the phone and motioned to my mother. "Larry thinks Gino is brain damaged like Larry Jr."

"What?" she gasped.

Then, my father, using an old, Italian euphemism for gay men, pulled on his ear lobe and whispered, "*Ricchione.*"

I had heard it used before, when my father saw certain people on TV whom he perceived to be gay. "David Bowie . . . *ricchione!*" "Liberace . . . *ricchione!*" Why tugging on an earlobe and using a word derived from the Italian translation for "ear" was meant for straight men to warn others that a homosexual was approaching, I have no idea. All I can think of is that gay men were the first to wear earrings aside from women.

"Oh, Jesus Christ on the cross," my mother said, lighting a cigarette.

"Al, I need you to help me here," Uncle Larry slurred. "Maybe a summer with you and A.J. and Jack and Frankie and the fishing and the sports can snap him out of it. Is that something we can do? I'm *FUCKED!*"

My father didn't hesitate.

"*Aspetta, aspetta* (wait, wait). What's today? Thursday. Come by this weekend, stay with us a couple nights, and then leave him here until school starts in September. We'll take care of everything. Don't worry about nothing."

"Oh, Alfred, I love you. I feel like a goddamned fool calling on my youngest brother for help."

"Larry, stop the histrionics. Chin up. Put down the vodka. You took care of my Rosalie for her first eighteen months while I was overseas. This is the least I can do. Larry, we love you and we all love little Gino. We're Benzas. We'll get through this."

By the time they had hung up, Lorraine, Aunt Mary, and I had all made our way out of our beds and were standing in the hallway.

"Your uncle Larry needs help with Gino," my father stated. "And that's what we're gonna do. It's gonna be a different summer for all of us, but this is what you do for *la famiglia.*"

We returned to our bedrooms more or less shell-shocked, none of us able to sleep. I could hear my mother and father talking in their bed as they settled back in.

"Jesus," my mother said. "What are the chances of having two queer sons? Poor Larry. I know the Lord works in mysterious ways, but—"

My father cut her off at the jump.

"Lilly, forget that horseshit about the Lord's *mysterious* ways," he said, dripping with the sarcasm of a determined atheist. "Let me tell you something: if your *boss* was that *mysterious*, you'd quit your fuckin' job."

3

SIDESHOW

I've had my dependency on various drugs over the years, but the biggest monkey I ever had to flip off my back was, undoubtedly, my sad reliance on Tums. Yes, Tums. The perfect little cylinder with the tightly wrapped foil paper that protected the smooth, chalky, white antinausea tablets neatly inside. From the time I was ten years old, I had them stashed in every room of the house. It was like I was getting ready for some apocalyptic agita. Eventually it got to the point I would never leave home without stuffing a roll in the right pocket of my pants.

Some might say my anxiety started on account of my mother having me in her late forties and, as a result, my grandparents and various aunts and uncles were dropping like flies. I quickly grew accustomed to death. I went to all their wakes. Most were open-casket affairs held at Scarpaci Funeral Home in Brooklyn. And my absolute first visceral memory as a child (I was two!) was sitting atop my father's shoulders as he walked us down a short, carpeted staircase and entered a room where I saw his mother laid out in a half-open box with big, gaudy sprays of flowers that Italians love to send. The bigger the mum, the deeper the grief. The room was empty except for him and me. I remember he told me how much my grandma Rosalia loved me—especially when I strummed my plastic guitar and sang to her "I Want to Hold Your Hand" on the stoop of our Bensonhurst walkup. Then he bent his upper body over the casket and told me to "kiss Nonna good-bye." And I still remember the feeling of my lips on her hard, life-less cheek and the sight of the pancake makeup she went out with. And, no, she didn't look "beautiful" or even remotely "peaceful" as everyone loves to say. She looked like she knew she was missing out on things.

I was two years old and I can recall huge chunks of that day. Even the smell is still jammed into the deep recesses of my nose. I personally don't think that fucked me up, but I can see a shrink having a field day with my early years.

If you ask me, it all started with being miserable with my fifth-grade teacher, Mrs. Kubissa. She was a close talker, and whenever she got eye level to reprimand me (which was a daily occurrence), I would almost gag on account of her cigarette, onion bagel, and coffee breath. I would be fine all morning, not a care in the world, eyeing all the pretty girls, but as soon as I saw her coming anywhere near my desk, I began fishing for my Tums like a tweaker digging for his glass pipe.

But then there was the day they weren't there.

I begged Mrs. Kubissa to let me go home—"It's across the *damn* street," I told her. "You can watch me the whole time."

She stood me up. "Does your mother put up with that language?"

"I'm telling you, Teach, in my house we say whatever the hell we need to say."

To her credit, she let me go. I popped four Tums, and the anxiety subsided. But in the weeks to come, I was granted a transfer to Mr. Gaggin's class across the hall. I simply couldn't live with that woman disciplining me while seeing the freedom of my home right outside the classroom window. Gaggin's room faced the back of the school, and he didn't smoke or drink coffee. In fact, he chewed Dentyne just like my father. And that's when I finally kicked the habit.

But, oddly enough, several hours after my father put down the receiver on the old rotary phone that strange night, I started turning the medicine cabinets upside down in search of some Tums. Never mind a whole roll. I would've settled for a few loosies that morning. But why the sudden change after being clean for two years? And then it hit me like a bull's-eye kick to the balls. I had heard both my father and my uncle plainly using the term "brain damaged" over the phone. And I was scared shitless. A few years earlier, my older cousin Terry grew so despondent over her husband leaving her, she took their beautiful little daughter, Maria, and stepped off the curb directly into oncoming traffic, hoping to take their lives. After a couple of cars ran them over, cousin Terry escaped a little banged up, but little Maria was left with several skull fractures. As usual, my father and mother offered to take care of Maria while her mother got counseling. All I remember of *that* summer was seeing Maria's pretty face topped off with tight white bandages and a turban of gauze. She was four years old; I was six, but I protected her like a piece of fine china. I even watched her as she slept.

Looking back, it's no wonder my demons came back again and demanded Tums, what with yet another damaged brain coming to stay with me.

After I had found an old roll in a winter jacket in the closet, I popped four of the chalky pills and paced around the kitchen in the general vicinity of my mother.

"What the hell are you eating?" she said. "Your lips are all white. Are you popping those friggin' Tums again? What's bothering you now?"

"What's bothering me?" I said. "I wanna know what it means that Gino might be brain damaged. I heard you and Daddy outside my room last night. Jesus, I could even hear Uncle Larry crystal clear coming through the receiver. He said, 'I'm afraid Gino is brain damaged like Larry Jr.'"

"Your ass!"

"No, Ma. I heard all of it. I even heard you lose your breath a little, and when I cracked open my door, I saw you make the sign of the cross. So what the hell was that about?"

She started laughing nervously, and whenever my mother went that way, I knew I had her dead to rights. "Tell me about Gino's brain, Ma. I deserve to know. I'm gonna be spending the summer with him. Is this brain damage gonna kill him? Is it catching? I wanna know."

"Rosalie!" my mother yelled for reinforcements. "Would you tell your brother why Uncle Larry is so concerned with Gino?"

"No," I said. "Why is he concerned with his *brain*? Is he retarded or something? What is going on? If there's any chance of me catching this brain damage, don't expect me to sleep with him or swim with him. I'm telling you right now."

I popped three more Tums.

"Will you stop with those fuckin' *Toms*," my mother said, staying true to her habit of mispronouncing the simplest of words.

"They're called *Tums*." I laughed.

"Whatever the hell. Just stop. They can't be good for you."

Oh . . . but exposure to brain damage *is*?"

"Rosalie, Lorraine, . . . please come in and help me here. This kid is raising my blood pressure through the roof; I gotta take a goddamn Librium, have a cigarette, and put my feet up in my chair."

Rosalie was headed out to the Italian specialty store to pick up food, so she was rushed. Lorraine, sweetly oblivious as she remains to this day, never saw any difference between Gino or even his older brother and other boys their ages. "I love Larry Jr.," Lorraine obliviously said. "I hope Gino turns out just like him."

That was enough for Rosalie to step in with some calculated force.

"A.J.," she said, "forget you ever heard the term 'brain damaged.' No one is brain damaged. It's not an illness. It's just . . . how can I put this . . . Jesus, Ma, why are you putting me through this?"

"Just tell me *something*," I begged her, looking around the room for anyone to chime in.

"It's just Gino is a different kind of boy than you are."

"We've always been a little different from each other," I said. "But now they're calling it brain damage, Ro. That sounds scary to me. And serious."

"No, no," she said. "It's just that right now Gino is not as rough a boy as you are. He's not as tough as you are, ya know? Don't forget, Uncle Larry went to work all day and Gino was left home most of the time with Larry, three sisters, and his mother."

That got me thinking. "So what? I get left home with you and NuNu, Aunt Mary, Aunt Mae, Arlene, and Mommy. So am I gonna come down with this brain damage too?"

At that point, my father dropped what he was doing to

swoop in and put an end to the discussion, which was his specialty. "Let's put this horseshit to an end," he said. "Your cousin Gino is going through a phase. He'll get over it."

"What's gonna stop me from going through a phase like that?" I asked my father.

"Me," he said. And that was that.

"Now make your mother happy and stop with the Tums already."

I still wasn't sure what they had on Gino, and to be honest, I knew they weren't telling me everything on the brain-damage front. So I stayed on my toes and decided to wait and see how he acted and interacted.

It didn't take long for me to start doing some summer math. Gino's arrival was gonna happen quickly, and his stay was gonna go on for roughly sixty-five days. And this was the terrifying summer before my neighborhood friends and I were all entering junior high school, and suddenly it wasn't solely going to belong to us anymore. Somehow—whether it was a tackle football game, a spontaneous fishing trip, flirting with the pretty girls next door or just some somber moments alone—I was going to have to work Gino into all those things. It wasn't like my cousin and I were strangers or didn't get along or anything like that. But there was no denying that as our wonder years went on, Gino was kind of peeling off in another direction. I didn't have a name for it. I just knew it was different. And over the hundred times or so we'd seen each other throughout the years, at weddings, funerals, and birthday parties—as well as the arduous, traffic-ridden trips my family took to spend some weekends at Uncle Larry's big house in beautiful, sunny Succasunna—about the most common thing we shared was having the same last name.

Jesus, those car rides to Jersey were hell. My father never raised his hands to me in his life, but those car rides amounted to the closest thing to child abuse that I can ever recall suffering. I wish I was lucky or tormented enough to block them out, but I never saw a shrink for help on this matter. But imagine me sitting on the hump seat in the back of a '64 Mustang (with no seat belts, mind you) and barely surviving the two-hour journey, as my parents chain-smoked Winstons with the windows *up* and the AM radio dial tuned to an oldies' station. To this day, if I hear even the opening of "Winchester Cathedral," I throw up in my mouth a little bit.

"Ma . . . can you and Daddy crack your windows when you smoke?" Lorraine would beg, above the eight-track stylings of Sinatra. "I swear, we're gonna die back here, and we're all about to throw up. *Please!*"

My father would visually clock us by adjusting his rearview mirror. "I'll roll them down a little bit, but you're gonna all freeze your asses off back there. Remember, the heater is shot and we can't afford to see Sal at the Sunoco station for another month or so."

"Fine, fine. We don't care."

I knew then what secondhand smoke was. Had I died, it would have been premeditated second-degree murder.

"Are we almost there yet?"

"Jesus Christ, A.J." My father would exhale. "We haven't even seen a sign for the GW Bridge yet. We got plenty of time to go. And that's if we don't hit traffic on the turnpike, which we will, because Jersey's highways are all laid out like your sister's ass." That was not a slight on Rosalie's or Lorraine's asses, it was just my father's interesting way of playing with words. Smushing fun in the face of good sense.

This was about as encouraging as it got, until those moments when my father would swing his right arm off the wheel and dig his strong fingers into our knees, hip bones, shoulders, stomachs, or whatever torturous, ticklish spot he could find while keeping his eyes on the road. Of course, all of us would be laughing and screaming for our lives, sometimes until the point of pissing ourselves. It was a reminder of how my father was equal parts tough and tender. He liked to break the boredom by busting balls.

The last Saturday in June of 1974 came at me like a shot. I was where I always was during the late morning hours—sitting three feet from the TV screen, drinking a giant grape soda, and eating a big bag of taco-flavored Doritos, while being engrossed in the *Soul Train* experience. I sat really close, not on account of bad eyesight but because at any moment—when my father would swing by the living room unannounced and see even a glimpse of Don Cornelius or the *Soul Train* line or word scramble—he'd convince me to change the channel in his own way.

"Look at you! Can't understand a fuckin' word they're saying, can you? But yet, you're watching this jungle-boogie bullshit."

"Dad, they're good. They sing better, they dance better—"

"*Who* dances better? None of those *coloreds* could hold Gene Kelly's shoes."

"It's different, Dad," I'd say. "They got a different way of doing things."

"Yeah. You know what else is *different*? Mowing the lawn is *different*. Go mow the lawn. I want us all to be out front when Uncle Larry and Gino get here, anyway."

My father wouldn't even have been home had it not been for his brother's arrival. He worked every damn Saturday of his life. So it's safe to say that every Saturday of *my* life, I was glued to *Soul Train*. It was church. Grape soda. Doritos. And becoming more and more enamored with black culture.

On the day of Uncle Larry and Gino's arrival, I eventually went outside and was rebounding and retrieving my brother-in-law Jack's free throws on our front yard basketball hoop when I spotted Uncle Larry's forest-green convertible Alfa Romeo speeding up the block and about to turn into our driveway. As usual, Uncle Larry had his leather racing gloves on and it was a toss-up as to what shined more brightly— his perfectly round, bald head or those bright, pesto-green, laughing eyes of his. In his youth, the pictures show that he would've given Paul Newman a run for his money. As he aged he was more a Yul Brynner type. Poor, clueless Uncle Larry was honking the horn and shouting for my father to come outside, and already—seconds into their stay—Jack had to lay down a simple rule we lived by without even thinking about it twice.

"Hey . . . Uncle Larry!"

"Hiya, Jack. You look great. How are you?"

"Listen," Jack announced. "You can't park here. You're on our basketball court. Can't play basketball with your car on the basketball court."

To Jack's credit, he was an elementary school gym teacher in Tuckahoe, New York, and—at various times in his tenure— had also coached the high school's varsity football, basket-ball, baseball, and soccer teams to winning seasons as well as county and state championships. He was also the high school's athletic director. Jack was a serious jock. I almost never saw him without a clipboard and a whistle.

Uncle Larry looked utterly confused. "We're just gonna get Gino's bags and I'll come back and move the car in a min-ute."

"Can't do it. We're shooting free throws. We shoot five hundred free throws every Saturday," Jack said. "You're break-ing our rhythm."

"You're not kidding," Uncle Larry said.

"Hey. No."

"Boy, oh boy . . . good luck, Gino," Uncle Larry said.

When Uncle Larry moved his car to the curb and they

approached the house, as my family spilled out to greet them, Jack shouted to Gino, who was carrying a couple of pieces of luggage.

"Hey, Gino . . . think fast," Jack said, as he tossed him the red-white-and-blue ABA basketball. "You're wide-open! Five seconds left. Knicks are down by one. Hit the shot. All you!"

Gino dropped his bags just in time to luckily catch the bounce pass. His pressing smile was as hard to look at as his lack of any idea of how to shoot a ball into a hoop twenty feet away. The ball looked like it weighed thirty pounds in his hands.

"Shoot it," Jack shouted. "Four . . . three . . . two . . . *shoot it!*"

With all his might, Gino sent up a shot that went over the backboard, bounced on the roof a few times, landed in the side yard, and came to rest in a small pile of dog shit courtesy of one of our mutts, Sonny or Pippen.

Jack broke the silence with a sharp sigh. "Hey . . . Knicks lose. Gonna be a long summer."

As all the members of our family were hugging and kissing Uncle Larry and Gino, I was so obsessed with my ABA basketball that I went and retrieved it from the pile, washed it off with the garden hose, and disappeared into the laundry room to get a towel and shine it as best as I could. But the ball had miles on it. It had been through epic, last-second moments between me and hundreds of imaginary opponents. When I wasn't trying to perfect a finger roll like Dr. J, I was performing the straight-up, climb-the-ladder jumper of his New Jersey Nets teammate, "Super" John Williamson. There were some nights, way past dinner, when the winter wind was whipping so hard that the zipper on my ski jacket made it sound like the metal collar and tags on the neck of Greg Lavazoli's vicious Doberman when it was loose and fast approaching. But I stayed with the play, and time and again, either Walt Frazier or Earl "the Pearl" Monroe helped me pull out a buzzer-beater before I bolted to the front door to actually see if it was my zipper that was scaring the piss out of me, or, in fact, Lavazoli's bloodthirsty dog. This was when Dobermans and German shepherds were the scariest things on four legs. Nobody had pit bulls yet.

Uncle Larry had taken the long route from Jersey that day and had cut through Manhattan's Lower East Side—where he and my father were raised—so he could get the best bagels and lox and even a handful of knishes at Yonah Schimmel on East Houston Street. (That was the only non-Italian food my father allowed in the house.) Meanwhile, my mother had matched him by putting together an incredible cold antipasto plate of salami, hard-boiled eggs, anchovies, olives, and roasted peppers, with fresh garlic, basil, and lemon zest spread all over it. And then there were mussels that we had picked several days earlier on a trip to a local marsh. They were steamed with the perfect amount of garlic, butter, and white wine. We ate them quickly as if they were potato chips. We only slowed down whenever one of us bit down on a small, dark pearl.

(And fuck Rachael Ray. None of these meals could be prepared in a flash. That would've been an insult to our family and guests. Some of these meals took two days to plan: my father had to harvest the mussels and my mother had to scrape off the barnacles, pull off the moss, and begin slaving over a hot, summer stove, flavoring them and watching over them until they were perfect and not too rubbery. Thirty-minute meal, my ass.)

When everyone finished their fair share of the mini Saturday feast, my father returned from Jack and Ro's backyard bulkhead—where he was proudly getting our boat ready for a fishing trip—he proudly told the men and boys that it was gassed up and ready for us to go out and bring home some fish.

"Larry," my father said. "Weakfish don't bite too often, but they're biting this week. And it's high tide. Let's get in the boat and go."

But Uncle Larry had other ideas. He wanted to make sure Gino had all the athletic equipment necessary to compete anytime a game broke out in the school yard.

"Alfred," my uncle said. "Lemme take A.J. and Gino to the sporting-goods store and buy a few things."

With the boat's engine running, and the high tide coming in quickly, that was the last thing my father wanted to hear. "Larry, Larry . . . not now. You're talking to a sailor. We'll miss the fish."

"Al, let me just do this," he said. "A.J., hop in the back of the car and tell me what I need to buy."

"Dad," I screamed over the boat's engine, "we're only going to Babylon. We'll be right back."

The inside of Babylon Sporting Goods on Main Street was something I had seen only through the back window of my father's car as we raced past it to see a movie at the RKO or buy some booze at the liquor store down the block from a man my father named Storio Longo because of the long stories he spun. We never stopped at the sports shop. We never had the money to buy me new equipment. My sports equipment was the stuff Jack would sneak home from his school's supply closet from time to time. It was weathered and used and all read PROPERTY OF TUCKAHOE HIGH SCHOOL. I never knew the smell of a new baseball glove or the perfectly tight seams of a Clincher softball. But when Uncle Larry parked in front of the place that Saturday in June and held the door open for Gino and me, you could've told me I had just landed on the moon.

I walked in the store and brushed my hand against everything. Even things I would never, ever own, like soccer nets or tetherball sets. Uncle Larry's green eyes lit up, while Gino's enthusiasm shrunk a bit. It was obvious he didn't know sports stores.

"A.J.," Uncle Larry said, "what does Gino need to have this summer to play with the rest of the boys?"

Talk about a loaded question.

The sales clerk stepped in and offered his help. But Uncle Larry declined, saying his nephew was going to choose what equipment he was going to buy. And then I heard a phrase, or the formation of words, that I had never heard in my life.

"Money is no object," Uncle Larry told the clerk, as I grabbed basketballs, footballs, baseball bats and mitts, and even some lacrosse sticks, even though I had never played the game.

Because we had always struggled financially throughout my childhood, I was used to hearing my mother yell into the phone at bill collectors, "If I write you a check it'll bounce from here to the moon." Or, even better, in her private moments when she was balancing our family's checkbook in the middle of the sun-splashed kitchen table, using her ninth-grade education and no calculator: "Well, if a trip around the world cost a nickel, we wouldn't be able to get off the friggin' block."

Now here I was with my uncle's open checkbook, bouncing out of the store and squeezing all the new merch into the back of his sports car.

"Thanks a lot, Uncle Larry," I said.

"No problem," he said. "As long as you have fun all summer. You hear me, Gino?"

Gino's head and soul were not quite aligned yet, as he fiddled with the radio and protected his hair from the wind whipping around the drop-top.

"Hey, Gino, what grade is for ten-year-olds in New Jersey?" I asked.

"I just finished fourth grade," he said.

"*Yech!* Fractions," I said.

"Yeah, they're not too bad," Gino said. "It's mostly adding fractions with unlike denominators when it gets tricky."

"Well, I'd rather go fishing than do fractions any day of the week," I said. "You ready to fish, Uncle Larry?"

"Your father is the fisherman in the family," he said. "But he'll teach me."

Right then and there I knew my uncle and Gino were in for trouble. When it came to people fishing on his boat, my father had the patience of a time bomb. He had a habit of telling you how to do things once before sending you off on your own. If you didn't catch on, he'd steal glimpses of you in moments of complete incompetence and just shake his head, take a long drag on his cigarette, and mutter to himself. Not tossing the anchor overboard correctly, or squeamishly baiting a hook, or leaving the clamming sacks back home were practically capital offenses.

By the time we got back and headed for the dock, my father was already waiting at the wheel with Lorraine's fiancé, Frankie, and Jack. We shoved off and meandered down the canals of my youth and into the slapping tides of the Great South Bay. The bay had been good to us for years. In the summer of 1974, the water was still clear enough that you could see straight to the bottom, fishing twelve feet deep or so. Maybe more. There were times when we were fishing for blowfish or flounder that we could actually see where the bigger fish were and we'd drop our lines right on top of them.

It was almost unfair. There were days when we'd fill a garbage pail full of fish in a couple of hours and we'd have to turn home because there was no more room to keep them on board. And sometimes we'd come home with so much that my mother would curse us.

"Oh, Jesus Christ! Who the hell is going to batter and fry all that damn flounder?"

"You are," my father said, "with a smile on your face."

And she always would. And whatever we couldn't eat would go to the neighbors up and down the block.

On this particular day, the water was choppy and Gino and I sat upfront with extra-large Windbreakers on to ward off the waves that were splashing into the bow of the boat. Behind us, beneath the steering column, my father would always keep a huge flask of Scotch on board and traditionally brought it out for the men to "toast" certain things during the journey. Whenever the first white cap was spotted, the flask was passed around to all the men and everyone said, "*A salute!*" The flask also came out whenever we spotted the first nice pair of tits on someone else's boat. "*A salute!*"

First sighting of seagulls following a school of bluefish? "*A salute!*"

First bite on someone's pole? "*A salute!*"

First fish on board? "*A salute!*"

I remember Gino got seasick in the first five minutes and Uncle Larry was three sheets to the wind before he dropped his line in the water. We had what we called a "pisswah" on board, which consisted of a blue-capped Clorox bleach bottle with the bottom cut out. This was what the men and boys could pee into before dumping their business overboard into the ocean. Uncle Larry never saw the huge, gaping hole in the bottom, so he promptly unscrewed the cap, stuck his prick into the bottle, and didn't realize he essentially peed all over the tackle box. Not too long after that display, my father turned the boat back around and headed near home for the flats to do some quick clamming, while his brother and nephew slept it off. Frankie and Jack snickered a bit, telling me I had a long road ahead if I was going to get Gino to toughen up and catch up to our standards.

"Gonna be tough jerking off to Pop's *Playboys* with Gino staying in your room," Frankie said. "Right, Jack?"

"Oh boy," Jack said. "I'll give him till August before his balls explode in his sleep."

"You guys are gross," I said. "I don't do that." I was lying, of course, as the burning cramp in my right forearm would attest.

Frankie leaned in real close as we headed back down the canal. "Who knows, maybe you'll be teaching Gino by August. You guys can have circle-jerk parties."

"Don't listen," I said into Gino's ear, as he was waking up. "These guys love talking about jizz."

"I don't even know what any of you are talking about," he said, his face flushed.

·   ·   ·

When we glided back to the dock, Gino and Uncle Larry had opened their bloodshot, salt-encrusted eyes and couldn't wait to get on terra firma. They were both sunburned, soaking wet, and traumatized.

"How was everything?" my mother asked, while admiring the fluke we caught and the clams we grabbed. She and my sisters had been busy blending the whiskey sours and putting out the dried sausage and cheese we always had waiting for us ashore. "What did Larry and Gino catch?"

"*Ugotz.*" My father laughed. "*Niente.*" Nothing.

She knelt down to be nearer his ear, as he was spreading out the clams, spraying them down with the garden hose, and organizing them by size. The big mothers for his homemade chowder, the littlenecks to be eaten raw, and the cherrystones to be steamed for *posillipo* sauce. "Al . . . are you gonna let Gino go again tomorrow?"

"Oh, yeah," he said. "He's going again. He's going with the ones who are staying." That meant, the next time the men were going to spend a day on the sea, Gino was gonna stay home with the women—the ones who were staying.

My father got right to work whipping up a fresh clam chowder while Jack and Frankie cut the fluke into fillet strips. Gino and I had the job of burying the fish heads deep into the garden compost.

"Do you do this after every fishing trip?" Gino asked me, gagging.

"Yep," I said. "But I don't think it does anything more than stink up the backyard."

"Oh . . . the expert," my father shouted through the kitchen window. "Is that what you think? Your father has the best earth in town. You'll see when I'm dead." He was feeling a little loaded, so I didn't answer back.

For reasons unknown to me, he always felt he made his point stronger by telling us how much more intelligent he'd become in our heads after he died. Come to think of it, maybe it was all his talk about death that made me chew through all those Tums.

While everything was cooking, my father took me, Uncle Larry, and Gino on a trip through his garden and grape arbor and eventually stopped at a very fertile peach tree that was the eyesore of my youth.

"Come here, Larry," my father said. "Look at what I did with this peach tree." He always presented it with a flourish, as if he were showing off a brand-new Picasso. "My son thinks he should be embarrassed of it."

Uncle Larry stood in the shade of the giant tree, which was bursting with too many peaches for us to ever eat, and marveled at it. "Oh, Al . . . Momma and Poppa would've loved to see this."

What they would have seen was my father's jerry-rigged invention that had the whole neighborhood slowing down as they drove by the house to sneak a peek at our side yard. My father would search for peach buds the size of almonds, at which point he'd take an empty wine bottle and guide the branch holding the bud all the way to the bottom of the bottle. A piece of duct tape would secure the tree branch inside the neck of the bottle, so that the entire tree branch would heavily droop and nearly rest on the lawn. At any given time during the spring and early summer, there were at least two dozen bottles on the tree, and for rubberneckers driving by it looked like nothing less than a twenty-foot-tall alien with wine bottles for hands and feet. A District 9 for winos. But in the weeks to come, as the small peach buds matured and broke free from the branches and came to rest at the bottles' bottoms, my father would remove the tape from the tree and take the bottles into his garage where his homemade wine operation was in full swing. Then he'd fill the bottles with the homemade stuff—be it white or red—and let it sit for a while so that the peach could fully ripen and offer itself, giving tremendous, bursting peach flavor with each pour.

Uncle Larry's green eyes got all weepy again. And that wouldn't be the last time the levees behind his eyes wouldn't hold on this trip. My father scooped up a couple of overripe peaches that had fallen onto the lawn, took his folding knife out of his pocket, and fed a few slices to him. My uncle's eyes welled up and rolled back into his head.

"*Dottore*," my father said, kissing his brother hard on the cheek, "why you cry?" He gently shoved him off toward our pool. "Go lay on the raft with your son while we finish cooking."

A day on the bay always had a way of knocking a man down early. But with the emotional baggage Uncle Larry had carried with him from Jersey—and with the hooch the men had on the boat—it was only a matter of time before each of us would fall off to a nearby lawn chair, pool raft, or couch for a little shut-eye. My father, despite all his aches and pains, was always the last man standing.

All the while he was cooking his chowder, the women crowded around him for clues as to how the boat trip went. They were asking questions that were out of their usual repertoire.

"What did the fluke bite on, Daddy?"

My father was terse with his answers while he taste tested the chow off a wooden spoon. "Squid and killie combo, Ro."

"Was it choppy out there?"

"A little windy, Mary, but we managed."

"Any trouble with the outboard? Did the boat conk out at all?"

"A couple times, NuNu. But your Frankie pull-started her right back up again."

My mother chimed in. "Is *all* the Scotch gone?"

My father put down the spoon and shut off the range.

"Yeah, baby! And we didn't spill a fuckin' drop. How's that?"

No one dared a follow-up question, but my father knew what everyone in the room was looking for: a status report on Uncle Larry's diagnosis of Gino.

After a few last swirls of the chowder, and another taste test, he turned to the girls. "Okay. The answer to the question all of you are dying to ask is, *yes*."

And with that, the ladies got closer and more quiet, huddling around my father and forming a human shield from the father and son floating on a raft in the shallow end of our pool.

My father began quietly. "That night on the phone, my brother Larry told me that 'a father knows.' He just knows, goddamn it. And now here's *your* father telling you the same thing my brother told me, all right? We know our boys more than our wives can ever know." When he spoke that adamantly, he'd point his finger in a way that was more threatening than a gun. And the thick, gold POPPA bracelet he wore on his wrist shook like thunder.

With that, the women slinked off to finish their dinner tasks: setting the table, plating the food, and feeding the men and boys seated before them.

"A father knows," my father repeated in exasperation to an empty room. "A father knows when his boy is different. Call it brain damage, call it whatever the hell you want. A father just knows. He knows." And then to put a period on it all, again in Sicilian. "*Ido sape.*"

My mother gently scratched him on his back. "Okay, okay . . . we'll figure it all out. It isn't the end of the world."

"It's goddamn close," my father said, before turning to the screen door and whistling for his brother and nephew to come inside. "Larry. Gino. Come. Everything's on the table."

In more ways than one.

Whenever my father was able to feed his whole family off the riches of the bay, he felt he was cheating the system. And whenever he could bring in vegetables from his garden for my mother to fry, sauté, roast, boil, or broil them, he acted as though he had fooled the world.

We never held hands and thanked the Lord for our food. My father had his way of saying grace.

"Larry, look at the table," he said. "We got the fluke with our hands, the clams with our feet, and the peppers and onions both come from the garden."

"Oh, this is just wonderful, Al," Uncle Larry said.

"Don't forget, you're drinking wine from the grapes we grow on the arbor between our house and Rosalie's house," my father said. "And the scallions all grow wild on the side of the yard, next to the garlic and potatoes. Later on, I'll show you what I did this year on the other side of the house."

My uncle just kept repeating, "This is wonderful," as my father got deeper into his proud dinner speech. As he was doing this, the women were busy making plates of food for the men and boys. It was never that my father demanded they do this, or that he even asked. It was just something my mother and sisters always seemed eager to do. And as the years went by, neither my father, Jack, nor Frankie ever grabbed for food. I could see this was foreign to Uncle Larry, who, at one point, reached for the red pepper flakes to scatter into his chowder.

"No, no, Larry, stop," my father said, calmly putting his hand on my uncle's arm. "NuNu, put some red pepper on your uncle's clam chowder."

"Okay, Daddy," NuNu said. "Tell me when to stop, Uncle Larry."

"I'll tell you what," my father went on, "I don't know why there are so many schmucks who buy all their fruit and vegetables at the store, when you can grow them and tend to it yourself. Not to mention, save a lot of money."

"You're right, Alfred," Uncle Larry said.

"Goddamn right I'm right," my father said, turning to my cousin. "Gino, remind me to show you the *melanzane* I pulled from the garden yesterday."

"Okay," he said, springing to attention.

"They're the most beautiful shade of purple; there's no name for it," my father said. "But, I'm also gonna show you some *gagootz* (zucchini) that are as long as your arm."

"That oughta be fun, right, Gino?" Uncle Larry chimed in.

"Yeah," Gino said. "I love big gardens."

This got my father going. Looking back, it's simple to see that he thought of himself as the provider, the ultimate disciplinarian, the decision maker, and the symbolic head of the family. Having Gino agree, even moderately, to see his garden works, was like putting on a war chest for my father.

He pushed his chair out and stood up. "Tomorrow morning," he stated, "A.J., you're going to let Gino carry the *sco-*

lapasta (kitchen colander), and we'll show him how fertile his uncle's earth is. Best on the block. Am I right?"

"Yes, Daddy."

"Yes . . . what?" he said.

"Yes. Best earth on the block. You're right, Daddy."

"You're goddamn right I'm right."

With the meal almost over and my father's homemade wine flowing freely, the mood was good and lively. But it was on these nights where the tumblers in his brain always seemed to dangerously give way and open up the safe to the soul of a hidden man. These were the moments when love was always served with a side order of danger.

Before everyone retired to their bedrooms, dead tired, my father held court and wouldn't rather be anywhere else: standing at the head of the table, with his jelly glass of wine, directing his family like Fellini would do with Marcello Mastroianni and the rest.

"Rosalie . . . tell your father how you saved those three kittens last week from the back of the bank parking lot. And how you fought off three colored girls on your own."

Or:

"NuNu, sing 'The Impossible Dream' from *Man of La Mancha*. But sing it in that fuckin' hysterical, terrible voice. Larry, listen. Lorraine is the prodigy who has absolutely zero range."

And finally:

"A.J., stand on the table and do your Georgie Jessel impression."

By the time all the bits were over and the brothers were bent over in laughter, it was obvious another big day with the family had been wrung dry.

My father and his brother remained at the table, while Gino and I sat with them and listened to stories of their youth.

My father said, "Boys, you have no idea how many times your grandfather stood up to make a family speech without realizing his zipper was down. Easter . . . Thanksgiving . . . Christmas Eve, forget about it. And he never wore underwear. So, you can imagine . . ."

Uncle Larry countered, "I think the old man knew it. He just wanted to piss off Momma!"

"Hey, Larry, remember when you dared me to hit you on the head with Momma's cast-iron pan?" My father laughed. "And I did it and knocked you down the stairs!"

"I still have the lump." Uncle Larry laughed. "Feel it!"

Both men traded stories like that for an hour until their sides hurt.

But just as suddenly, as if the men could no longer deny Gino's trip in the first place, the mood went somber. The brothers lit up a couple more cigarettes, downed a few more wines, and decided it was time to size up Gino and me.

Right before they started, my father told me to flip through the records inside the dining room stereo console and "put on some *good* music from *real* musicians." I knew this was a test I had taken many times before, but I knew I had better get it right with my uncle and cousin present. I fingered past my sister's collection of Chicago, the Rolling Stones, and the Beatles albums before stopping on Benny Goodman. I dropped the needle on "Sing, Sing, Sing" and the brothers delightfully approved. That was my go-to song whenever I wanted to soothe my father. I remember being ten years old and my father telling me I had to know the names of all the men of the Swing Era before he allowed me to know a single, shallow thing about Mick Jagger and those guys. There were nights when he would sit with a Scotch at the head of the table—while all the women went to bed—and he would test me on each song.

"Who's on trumpet?" he'd say.

"Harry James."

"And what do they call him?"

"The Hawk."

"Good. Good boy."

"Now, who's banging them drums?"

"Oh, that's easy," I'd say. "Gene Krupa."

"Don't get cocky. Piano?"

"Teddy Wilson?"

"Nice. But you pulled that out of your ass. Dare I ask, who's going for a ride on the vibes?"

"That would be . . . Lionel Hampton."

"You're getting good," he'd say. "Last question: Who's the bad, bad man on the saxophone?"

"That's easy," I'd say. "The Italian guy . . . Sam Butera!"

"Good job, buddy boy" he'd say, as I climbed on his lap. "You gotta know who's who, before you know what's what." And then, in a proud whisper, "There are no Rolling Stones without the Benny Goodman Orchestra. You understand what I'm saying? Everybody takes and steals from someone else until they find out who they really are."

"Yeah, I get it, Dad. You're right."

With Uncle Larry and Gino present, I lined up Louis Prima and Keely Smith and Frank Sinatra as dutifully as any DJ who truly understands his audience. Mind you, as the brothers are wonderfully singing along, Gino is lost in my display of blind devotion and discipline. It's obvious to me he's never heard this music in his life and watching his father come alive is oddly funny to him. I gave him a wink and we share a quick laugh.

"Daddy, you're a terrible singer," Gino finally said, as his father tries to hit a Louis Prima high note toward the crescendo end of "I Ain't Got Nobody."

"A soprano, your father is not," my father said to Gino.

"Gino, give me a break here," Uncle Larry replied. "No one can sing like Louis Prima."

"He's just yelling," I interjected over the old men's joy. "It's not *really* singing."

"He's saying beautiful things in Sicilian," my father assured us. "Things a young boy can't understand. But one day you'll sing along with him too."

With the needle skipping at the edge of the thirty-three,

Uncle Larry perked up in his chair, walked to a big bag he had brought with him, and fished out a Jackson 5 album and held it up in an ecstasy I secretly shared with him.

"Al," Uncle Larry proudly began, "how much have you listened to these boys? The young one is amazing. A pure genius."

My father put up his hand.

"What's the matter?" Uncle Larry asked. "Have you really *listened* to their music?"

"I've listened enough to know I've listened too much."

I couldn't grab the album out of Uncle Larry's hand fast enough and search for some of my favorite songs. I hadn't seen a Jackson 5 album up close. My father wouldn't allow it. Just like he wouldn't allow my sister Rosalie to buy an Elvis record during the 1950s.

"Alfred . . . you can't mean that," Uncle Larry continued. "This kid is going to be the biggest star in the music world."

"Whose fuckin' music world?"

I dropped the needle onto a very young Michael Jackson singing "Who's Lovin' You."

"Al," Uncle Larry went on. "Would you just listen to that? These are all kids. A whole family of beautiful kids who sing and dance like nobody else."

"Wow," I yelled over to Gino, "I remember seeing them do this on *Ed Sullivan*."

Gino looked as though my remark might start a war, but I didn't think my father heard it over his bubbling anger.

"One black kid is cute, two are called trouble, and five means you got a fuckin' riot on your hands," he said.

"Dad, Uncle Larry is right," I said, taking advantage of the soft side he reserved for my sometimes disagreeing with him. "Cathy Krager let me kiss her in gym class while we were dancing to 'Rockin' Robin.'"

"Another sweet song," Uncle Larry said.

"Krager's an Irish name or, even, German," my father thought aloud. "You want a crazy mick or kraut wife?"

The speed and honesty of this discussion was whirling around Gino's enthused head. "They let you guys kiss in school?"

"No. No way. But I like her, and I just went for it. The first time I kissed her was kindergarten," I said. "I remember we were finger painting at the time . . ."

"And how'd that go?" my father said.

"She ran out of class and cried all the way to the nurse's office."

"Now she sounds German. Very cold people," my father said. "Do yourself a favor, stay away."

"Alfred, you're going to tell me you didn't find that song beautiful?"

"I'm looking at the bigger picture, Larry. I'm saying that something's off with this kid," he cryptically said. "That kid looks like he's *been* here before. Look deep inside his eyes. He's hurt, Larry. He's not happy. Whenever an eight-year-old can sing the blues better than a grown man, you gotta ask yourself where has he felt that pain before?"

"Ah, come on," Uncle Larry said.

"No, no, no. And I'll tell you where he's felt that pain," my father said. "At home."

"What's the use?" my uncle said. "I'm right, but I can't win."

After an awkward pause, and before the next song on the album could even begin, my father shot me a quick look to get back to *his* music. "Put on Frank again and then you guys go hit the rack so my brother and I can shoot the shit a little."

Before both men sent us off to bed, Uncle Larry was gentle with his kisses and hugs and pats on the head. My father's send-off included a relentless bout of tickling; a mock prize fight; hard, loud kisses that roused the dogs from sleep; and a promise that "tomorrow is gonna top today."

After being sent to bed, Gino and I had a few laughs before he passed out in his cot right next to my single bed. With no TV in the room, the only entertainment I had was eavesdropping on the conversation downstairs. Amid countless replays of "My Way" and "That's Life," I heard the brothers make promises to each other through their tears. It wasn't easy, and I had to stand real still and cock my head just right, but I swear I could make out the sounds of the twisted emotions of two devoted brothers that night. Sinatra was loudly singing, "But if there's nothing shaking come this here July / I'm gonna roll myself up in a big ball . . . and die." But what bit deeper into my ear were the sniffles, hard hugs, and whispered promises my father and uncle shared as the giant consoled stereo huffed out and my big old house went silent for the night.

4

COME AND GET YOUR LOVE

Even the sun had a hard time beating my father out of bed in the morning. I could hear him shuffling around at five or so, rifling through the newspapers, sucking down coffee, lighting a cigarette, talking to the dogs, and doing all sorts of stuff in and out of the house that would weigh heavily on the kind of day we were headed for. As much as I wished to fall back into a deep sleep, there was something so comforting about the noises he made on an early Sunday morning. I looked forward to them as much as I did sleep. Whether it was hearing him squirting lighter fluid into his silver Zippo lighter or going in and out the kitchen screen door or backwashing the pool filter, it was all music I stayed half asleep to. He would arrange the pots and pans we would need later on that day for dinner, tune the old AM radio to *Goombadah* Joe Rotolo's Italian music countdown. He would get the dogs into a tizzy, rolling them over and rubbing their bellies until they panted for their lives.

He was a father. He had a day off from work. He made noise. And it was a symphony to me.

I heard him talking through the slats of the guest room door my uncle was still asleep in to give him some shit.

"Paging Dr. *Pazzo* (crazy). Paging Dr. *Pazzo*. You have patients who need your assistance. Dr. Pazzo . . . *che cosa stai faciendo?* (What are you doing?) *Stai ancora dormendo?* (Are you still asleep?) *Sei ancora ubriaco?* (Are you drunk?) Paging Dr. Pazzo . . . *dove sono le sfere.* (Where are your balls?) *Scuso, Dr. Pazzo . . . possiamo anche avere della palline?* (Pardon me, do you even *have* balls?)

"Jesus *Christ*," Uncle Larry said. "You can't possibly be awake and fine with everything we drank last night. What the fuck are you made of?"

"*Sono forte*," my father said, loudly. (I am strong.)

"What are you cooking for breakfast?"

"*Cazzo* (cock), *calcazelle* (squash), *l'uove* (eggs)."

"Oh, my favorite. I'm coming. Gimme a minute."

It would be a couple of hours before Gino and I woke up and wandered downstairs, but I slept with more comfort knowing that was the man I hung my whole day upon. We had a small dish of a pepper-and-egg omelet he had prepared for us and a quick chocolate egg cream before I checked the papers to see the Yankees box score from the night before. They had lost. Again.

"Jesus Christ," I said. "When will the Yankees stop sucking?"

"Who knows," said my father, who was at the sink with Uncle Larry, washing some peaches that had fallen to the ground during the night. "Makes no difference anyway. Unfortunately, you'll never see the Yankees of *my* day. *Those* were ballplayers. Am I right, Larry?"

"Oh yeah."

"They were dignified; they had class. They wore god-damned suits and ties to the ballpark. Nobody had a friggin' Afro pick in their hair. And that's what you got now. Any-how . . . there'll never be another Joe DiMaggio."

"No. Never happen," Uncle Larry chimed in.

"He was a pretty ugly guy," I said, drawing a laugh from Gino. "I don't understand what Marilyn Monroe saw in him."

"I don't really know who this *Jody Maggio* is," Gino said. "But no one was as gorgeous as Marilyn. She was just so, so beautiful. So sad what happened to her. I cut out a whole bunch of pictures of her and glued them to the covers of my schoolbooks."

A flash of exasperation and embarrassment flushed my uncle's face as he leaned into my father and said, "You see what I'm working with here?"

"*Non tu preoccupare* (don't you worry)," my father whispered. "Watch."

Then, back to us, my father said, "Well, that was a situation Joltin' Joe didn't know he was getting himself involved in," my father said.

"What do you mean?" I said. "What was wrong with it?"

At this point some of the women of the house had meandered into the kitchen and caught a whiff of our conversation. My mother was pouring herself a cup of coffee. Aunt Mary was reading the paper's comic strips—*Dondi* was her favorite. And NuNu had scooped up one of our five cats onto her lap.

"What did I miss?" my mother said, grimacing at the first sip of coffee.

"My son wants to know about DiMaggio and Monroe," my father said.

"Be careful, Al," she said. "Larry, help me please. It's too early in the morning and too early in their lives to get into this."

"Hold on, Lil," Uncle Larry said. "A.J. is just curious."

"Basically . . ." my father began, "Joe didn't know what he was headed for. And Gino is right—Marilyn was beautiful. She was also very powerful in the movie studio system. But, ah, you know . . ."

My father at a loss for words? This threw me for a loop.

" 'But, ah, you know' . . . what?" I said.

"Maybe Jody Maggio knew she was too beautiful for him?" Gino offered.

"Oh, Jesus," Uncle Larry huffed. "Gino, it's *Joe Di-Maggio*. His name isn't *Jody*. He's the greatest ballplayer of our time. I've told you about him. I know I have." My father pinched his brother's cheek, as if to reassure him.

Gino kind of shrugged his shoulders.

"What's the big mystery here, Dad?" I said.

"Joe married a *hua*, but he didn't know it," my father said. "Nicest guy in the world, best ballplayer you'll ever see, got taken for a ride by a fuckin' *hua*."

"What's a *hua*?" I asked.

"Al . . . please watch what you say here," my mother went on.

"You dug a pretty deep hole for yourself, Alfred," Uncle Larry said, laughing a little.

"A *hua* is a woman who sleeps around. She goes from one man to another."

"A slut," I offered. "Everyone called Sue Whalen a slut in fifth grade ever since she let five guys go into the closet with her when we played Seven Minutes in Heaven at Marlon Houseman's house party."

"Yes, exactly, more or less, like her," my father said. "Monroe slept with President Kennedy, his brother, the mobster Sam Giancana, Paul Newman, Howard Hughes, Rubirosa—"

"All right, Al," my mother interrupted. "We don't know for sure—"

"Frank Sinatra got in there; Dean Martin, Peter Lawford. I think the whole fuckin' Rat Pack except for Sammy Davis, but who knows, that one's got an eye for white women."

"Probably his good eye, right, Dad?" I said, drawing a laugh from the adults.

"Maybe it's all not true," Gino said. "People think they know everything about some people and they really know nothing."

"No, Gino," my father calmly said. "This is based on facts. You could look it up." He turned to my mother: "Lilly, you read the rags. What do they say? What does your girl, there, Rona Barrett say on this matter?"

My mother, as usual, wanted to muzzle my father. "All I remember reading is that they said she was a dirty woman. You know . . . she ate in bed and left the plates under the covers. She left her room messy."

"She was a pig," my father said. "And what else?" Being that he was an ex-undercover cop in the 1950s, my father had that attribute that all law enforcement has—they ask only questions to which they already know the answer.

"Well, I've read she didn't wear any underwear and sometimes stayed in bed for days," my mother said reluctantly.

"Exactly," he said. "And that's when guys like Milton Berle, Yul Brynner, Mickey Rooney, John Huston, Tony Curtis, Marlon Brando, and Monty Clift would swing by."

Gino and I were just trying to make sense of all this. This entire diatribe, all because I simply lamented that the Yankees sucked in 1974.

"The studio knew she was like this. They fed her drugs; they sent the guys over. They knew they had a *putana* (slut) on their hands. But she was a *putana* who made them millions. So in a way, it's very sad what they did to her. Anyway . . . that was what Joe DiMaggio walked into."

"That's sad," Gino said after a long pause.

"What are you gonna do? That's the way the cookie crumbled," my father said.

The rest of that Sunday morning stayed pretty somber as Uncle Larry readied to leave. He had a private talk with Gino in the backyard, telling him he was basically with us so his mother, my aunt Geneva, could recover from the hysterectomy she'd recently undergone.

"And Mommy needs rest?" Gino asked, his eyes bubbling with tears.

"Yes, Gino," Uncle Larry went on. "And the one main thing the doctor said is that your mother doesn't need to be on her feet every day. Getting up and down all day wouldn't be good for her recovery. She needs to get better."

Gino was getting a bit nervous with the blunt news and the realization that for the next two months or so, he wouldn't be seeing his family. He would be all ours. And our respective homes were worlds apart—his being as quiet as a silent auction, and ours as calamitous as a casino.

"But I could be quiet, Dad. I'll do things for myself. I'll be good."

"Oh, Gino," Uncle Larry said, sweeping him up into his arms. "You're always a good boy, and you know how much I love you. We talked about this. Just a few weeks with Uncle Al and Aunt Lilly and before you know it, you'll be home again."

Gino squeezed his father tighter around his neck.

"And when you get home, your mother will be healthy and you'll feel better and better about yourself having spent time with your cousins." He kissed Gino several times on his head.

Uncle Larry saw my father staring through the dining room screen door and raised his eyebrows in a manner of desperation and concern. And when my uncle turned his body from the house, we could now see Gino's tear-stained cheeks from the various spots we were all stationed at inside the house. Suddenly I was able to make a deeper connection between this tender scene and the frantic, late-night phone call my father fielded just a few nights earlier. What that connection was, I hadn't yet figured it all out yet.

Before we all went to the front yard, my father had packed Uncle Larry's sports car with some clams, a bundle of fresh basil and mint, a peach tree sapling, and several bottles of wine that had a matured peach at the bottom. "It's better to wait a few weeks, so that the peach can give off its flavor," he told my uncle.

"Well, we'll see how long that lasts," Uncle Larry said. "I think I may need this tonight."

We all hugged and kissed my uncle good-bye, my mother going last. "Larry," she whispered. "Don't you worry about this little boy. We'll take care of him as if he's ours. Everything will work out." She pulled him closer. "I don't care what your brother says, God works in mysterious ways."

"Lilly, there's no one like you," Uncle Larry said, choking

up. "And there's no one like my brother. I know you'll do what you can. I love you."

"Larry," she said. "We love you too. With all our heart, our soul, and our guts."

As was somewhat of a custom whenever relatives left, my father liked for us to break the sadness with a dose of insanity. "Always leave them laughing," was something he drilled into me. On that particular morning, Rosalie teased her thick black hair sky-high and placed newspaper over her two front teeth. My mother wore a ridiculous sombrero. Frankie wore a kung fu getup and whirled around his nunchakus; Jack held over his head two Spanish swords he had bought in a garage sale, and my father bent over backward to moon his brother as his car pulled out of the driveway. The bunch of us yelled "Ciao, ciao" at the top of our lungs, and Uncle Larry screeched away with happy tears streaking his cheeks.

Gino, however, had different tears on his face.

"Don't worry, cuz," I said. "It'll be all right."

"No, I'm fine," he said. "It's just allergies."

Once the costumes were put away, my father quickly mapped out the day. He always felt the sun and the bay were the best ways to make everything fine. That's where he found his happiness, and he gently pushed that medicine on us for years. And, over time, we all became followers. Now it was Gino's turn to take his hit.

I don't recall how my father ever found our Long Island home, while we were cooped up in that two-bedroom walkup in Bensonhurst. It was an hour east on the Belt Parkway and the Southern State Parkway, and then he had to know to get off at the Robert Moses State Park exit some fifty miles later. It had to be the water that drew him off the exit ramp and down a long, straight street called Snedecor, which took its name from the Indian tribe that once inhabited the area. When we first moved there, in 1965, there weren't too many standing houses that separated our home from the beautiful and inviting Great South Bay. We were mostly surrounded by dirt lots and big, weeded hills in every direction. But that meant we could see the Captree Bridge from anywhere on our lawn, outside our bedroom windows, and even from the kitchen. It was beautiful and majestic and seemed brand-new. And there was a magic about it, knowing that virtually everyone driving on it was headed for the beach or for a fishing trip or for a boat ride to Fire Island. And who's ever in a bad mood when those are the choices?

On some days, my father would leave the house shirtless, wearing just a swimsuit and a shoulder holster carrying a huge knife. He was barefoot, and a large shark's tooth necklace hung from his neck. In his hands, he carried an empty potato sack, a folded lawn chair, a fishing pole, and a small tackle box of assorted hooks, weights, bobbins, knives, and line. These days, that getup would probably have a neighbor dial 911. Or at least 311. But back in the late sixties and early seventies, he got away with it. He still cut a great physique while looking handsome and menacing at the same time. Looking back, he had Robert De Niro's vibe before De Niro was old enough to have it himself.

That afternoon, he had pulled my mother aside and told her of his plan to take Gino and me to the water. This was another way of getting a bead on Gino, who was too young to possess a poker face. But there were times, nonetheless, when he was virtually unreadable.

"Give me some time with the boys," he told her.

"What are you gonna do?"

"I'm gonna do whatever the hell I gotta do. You got any better ideas?"

"No," she said, "I wish I had an easy answer. I wish I could help somehow."

"Lilly, you wanna help? Just cook," he said.

"All right, all right. Maybe you want a nice marinara sauce for later?"

"Nah, let's go with a meat sauce. You got any veal?"

"Veal? *Veal*," my mother said. "Who's got money for veal this week?"

"Oh, for chrissakes," he said. "Just keep it beef and pork then. Bust my balls over veal, now?"

"Just go enjoy the water. What are you gonna bring home?

"I dunno. I never done this before. Hopefully a changed boy."

They kissed and my father whistled for Gino and me to follow him down the street, where in less than half a mile, the road eventually gave way to a beach, and the beach presented the Great South Bay before us. For Gino, who was coming from a nicely established upper-middle-class neighborhood in Succasunna, New Jersey, this little walk—peppered with dirt hills, interesting pieces of driftwood, and dried beds of seaweed—must've felt like being dumped into a trip to Castle Rock in *Lord of the Flies*.

My father was always first in the water, without so much as testing its temperature with a toe. He'd been doing this for years and knew exactly where to bring us. I had taken this walk with my father a hundred times before. We did this more often than tossing a football, hitting a baseball, or kicking a soccer ball. I guess he felt Jack and Frankie would pick up that slack, while nobody could teach me the wonders of water better than he could. So, for us, that walk to the bay was like church. When he felt he found the right spot—which usually meant he felt lots of clams stuck in the sand beneath his feet—he beckoned us in. I made sure I stuck real close to Gino, for fear he'd bolt back up the beach and give up on getting involved. Gradually we got deeper in the water until we were about waist-high. We walked the crystal clear flats of the bay floor, our little legs dragging through sea grass a foot high—which held a fear of the unknown like nothing else I knew. Gino, to my amazement, was keeping step with me—both of us holding one hand on our chests and the other guarding our nuts. We gently stepped down our bare feet on unknown hard knots of sea life and, worst of all, crabs of every variety—blue claws, spider crabs, and sometimes the prehistoric horseshoe crab. Two summers earlier, my father had instituted the "no socks" rule, denying the safety provided by a simple tube sock. He demanded I go in barefoot, insisting the tiny cushion of cloth on my sole would deny me the instant clue that I was undeniably stepping on a clam. I had gotten somewhat used to it, but now Gino had to abide by it as we trudged on, inch by inch, to get right next to my father. I couldn't keep count of the sea creatures—small fluke, lazy eels, schools of silverfish, and various kinds of sea cucumber we unexpectedly awoke from slumber until we reached him.

In those few seconds when my father would duck underwater for a clam or two, I could see Gino taking in the expanse of the bay and the little fish that were eerily breaking water all around us. When we were finally standing next to him, my father would make this wondrous face that gave way to a sentence I had heard many times over the years with him. "I got a triple header here," he said. "I have two under my right foot and one under my left."

"But Dad, the grass is *really* high . . ."

"Stop with the grass already. Stop. Listen to me," he said. "A.J., you hold on to the belt loop on the right side of my shorts. Gino you grab a hold of a loop on the left side."

We were both stationed to go but petrified at what we'd uncover under his feet. After all, those lumps weren't always clams. "On the count of three," he said. "I want you boys to exhale and use my legs as pillars until you reach directly under my feet and come up with the clams, *capiche*?"

"What if there's a crab down there?" I said.

"A.J., if I'm not stepping on a crab, you aren't going to step on a crab."

"Wait!" Gino said. "What's a *pillar*?"

"He just means use his legs like they are long poles that we climb down," I said.

It was more than just the threat of grabbing a crab, once I got down to my father's feet. It was the baitfish swimming between my legs, the snappers darting to our left and right, and the piles of sargasso-like seaweed my father would part as if it were his own little Red Sea. The bay was teeming with so much life to the point where it scared the *life* out of me.

I gave it one more shot. "Dad, the grass is *really* thick and high here," I said. "Maybe we should find another spot."

"Yeah . . ." Gino said. "I'm with A.J."

"You two gotta stop," he said. "If you're stepping on grass, that's good. It means no one has been there before. There's probably a lot more than three clams around here. Try three dozen."

My father hated to stand on a clam too long. It was as if he believed all the other clams nearby would suddenly get unstuck and disappear from the area. And so the clock in his head meant more than the one on his wristwatch. "Come on, boys," he said. "I'm not trying to keep you here all day. Let's just get a few dozen clams, maybe a dozen blue-claw crabs with the fishnet and head home."

Gino and I were set to go under on the count of three. At *one*, we started laughing. At *two*, we took deep breaths. At *three*, I was the only one of us who went under and swam down the murky sight of my father's leg until I grabbed a hold of his heel. I took a blurry peek at where Gino was standing, but I could see that he was nowhere to be found on the left leg, so I went to work. I had forgotten to exhale, so my ass was floating up to the surface like a bobbin, and I felt my father slam my body down into the water. Before I knew it, I was lying on all that mysterious sea grass, but I had loosened two of the clams. One was a small cherrystone, the other a monster chowder clam, which was really dug in deep. I could hear my father above the water, shouting instructions to me. "To the right, to the right!" Before I lost all my air, I finally pulled the big clam free from the muck and came up begging for a gulp of fresh air.

"Here." I coughed. "Here's two. That second one was so deep."

I was breathing like I had just swam in the Olympics.

"*Calma, calma* (calm down)," my father said. "You were underwater eight seconds for chrissakes."

"You didn't go," I said to Gino.

"I can't do it. I'll never do it. I'm sorry," Gino said, to my surprise.

Though my father was visibly disappointed at Gino, his biggest concern at the moment was the clam under his left foot. "Come on," he said. "This clam I got here isn't gonna swim up to the top and jump in the sack, A.J. Do it again."

And that's the way it went that Sunday afternoon. My father stomping on clams and basically doing a movement similar to the Twist to loosen the grip on the sea's bottom, and me swimming down his legs to dig them out and toss them in the sack. We had three dozen in no time. Gino was getting more and more distant with each minute we spent out there and more and more insecure at my success and enthusiasm.

"I'm sorry you didn't try harder, Gino," my father said. "I thought you'd get the hang of this fast *and* start doing it *better* than my A.J." It was a lie he knew he had to tell.

"I never even went swimming in a bay before, let alone clamming," Gino said. "I'm getting a little tired anyway, Uncle Al."

"That's okay. You'll do it next time. We got enough clams. Let's take a little walk by the grassy areas and see if we can't grab a few crabs."

Grabbing crabs in the flats was easier than clamming, but you had to be really fast with the net. That's why my father counted on our eyesight, while he would be the one doing the actual catching.

We placed our bag of clams on the beach and then set out to search for crabs that liked to crawl in the really shallow, grassy waters once the tide went out. We did this for an hour or so, with the sun beating down on our backs and the mosquitoes and deerflies biting our legs from time to time, but it was worth it. The crabs weren't too big in early summer—you had to wait until September to catch the real monsters—but every so often you'd find a "big mutha," as my father called them. And on the good days, they were too slow to escape his skills with the net.

Gino didn't want too much of this either, but he trudged on long enough until we had our haul in place. Three dozen clams and one dozen crabs in a little over an hour.

"Not bad, boys," my father said. "We stuck it out and now we have ourselves a couple nice appetizers to go along with your mother's sauce."

"Uncle Al, your fingers are bleeding," Gino said.

"That happens. It ain't like these crabs *wanna* go in a bucket. Sometimes you gotta rip them off the net and get them in."

My father let me hold the sack of clams over my back the whole way home. Gino carried the bucket of crabs, which were alive and moving and a bit challenging for a first-timer. And it scared the hell out of him with each step.

"You can do it, Gino," my father said. "Uncle Al has faith in you."

"Yeah, come on, cuz," I teased. "They only crawl out of the pail and onto your arm once in a while."

"Please," Gino shrieked. "I'll drop them right now!"

Before we got home, as we walked past the weeded hills of plots of land that would one day be houses, my father told us to drop everything and follow him. "I see some great stuff behind that little hill," he said. He pulled a folding knife out of his tackle box and got right to work on the vegetation that was growing wild. Most everyone else would've walked right past this stuff, but not my father. Here it was, modern-day Long Island, and I'm watching my father living off the land like a pioneer. Obviously, it wasn't just the bay he gratefully took from. He could scan the foliage in the many lots near our home with his sharp, knowing eyes and recognize the shape and veins of a leaf, the color of a berry, the gentle slope of a stem crowned with flowers. He cut dandelion leaves and wild pansies. He knew what mushrooms were okay to pick and put in the pan. He took in every life-form around us and it was all one giant salad to him.

By the time we got home and dumped the haul onto the pavement in the backyard, the sun had dried us off already. We jumped in the pool to get the salt water off our bodies and watched my father arrange the clams by size. He handed a bundle of greens to my mother, who had been busy whipping up blended whiskey sours and arranging a plate of cheese and dried sausage for him. And later on he dumped the crabs into a huge pot of water with seasonings and placed it on the hot barbecue grill.

Gino swore he could hear the live crabs make noises as they boiled.

"It sounds like they're screaming for their lives," he said to me, standing by the heat of the grill.

At this point I was a little upset with Gino's lack of getting involved. "Crabs don't talk," I said. "Quit worrying about them."

"Well," Gino muttered, "they don't sound happy, anyways."

The lazy Sunday ended with a family feast of linguini

with clam sauce, chicken *scarpariello*, steamed broccoli rabe with garlic and oil, and that salad my father picked on the way home from the bay. Jack and Frankie ripped apart the crabs in addition to the dinner before us.

"*Mangia, mangia* (eat, eat)," my father said to everyone.

"Yeah," my mother countered. "There's plenty of food. There's too much food."

"No such thing, Lilly," my father said. "Whatever we don't finish, we'll give to the neighbors."

Jack peeped up. "Ahhh, Pop, we'll finish it. Don't worry at all. Delicious. Perfect. None of this is going anywhere but staying here."

But Gino pushed his food around, not eating much. I watched as he had a couple of swirls of pasta but basically mushed his clams into a bunch of bits and disguised them inside the salad. The chicken was untouched. My father had to explain how hard my mother worked in the kitchen before Gino finally nibbled a little on some bread dipped in red sauce.

"There are kids starving in Europe," my father said. "There should be nothing left on these plates except your forks."

Being "brain damaged" was one thing. Pushing my mother's food away was a completely different story. My father took his last gulp of wine and trudged off away from the head of the table.

"I'll be in the garage, Lilly."

He had nothing important to do in the garage, except allow for his absence to make a point.

I knew I hadn't done anything wrong, so I grabbed Gino by the back of his shirt, practically waking him from a coma, and took him into the living room to watch some TV. My sisters and I had a silly thing we did—I don't want to say a tradition, but we did it almost every Sunday night. We would turn on Mutual of Omaha's *Wild Kingdom*, starring its old host, Marlin Perkins, and make fun of all the corny stuff he said about zebras, tigers, and bears. One thing that drove us crazy was how the producers would do their sneaky segues, tying the commercials to the subject of the show. The producers would have Perkins saying something like "Just as the polar bear protects her cubs, you can protect *your* children with an insurance policy from Mutual of Omaha. . . ." Oh, it drove us nuts.

So we had our own version of doing it. We'd lower the sound during the commercials and volley funny bits across the room. "The owl can turn its head almost 360 degrees, but it can't puke pea soup like that crazy bitch Regan MacNeil in *The Exorcist*!"

My sisters would laugh and laugh. "Stop it. . . ."

I'd go on, looking over my shoulder for my mother. "In our next episode, the owl's mother sucks cocks in hell."

This got a rise out of Gino. It was a language and a type of laughter I don't think he'd heard too much before. I saw *The Exorcist* when I was eleven years old, simply because I asked my father. He took me with him to see it one night but told me we'd leave the minute I covered my eyes. So I made sure to keep my eyes glued to the screen and my hands by my side. Gino, on the other hand, had never heard of the classic horror film.

"Wait." He laughed. "Who pukes pea soup? What are you guys laughing about?"

My mother spoke up from the hallway. "Never mind that movie, Gino," she said. "My son is full of shit. He's been chewing Tums ever since he saw that friggin' film!"

"That's a lie, Ma! She's lying, Gino, I swear."

When my father came out of the garage an hour later, we were all expecting the worst. But in the midst of his liberal parenting, there were nights and times that demanded certain disciplines and structure. Sunday nights, for my sisters and me, had always been about watching our father collapse into his recliner and our giving him a head-to-toe rubdown to get ready for the workweek. This night, as it turned out, was no different. But the stakes were a bit higher because we were working with somebody new.

"Your poppa needs a rubdown," he said to the heap of human laughter we all were at that moment. "But not just any rubdown. I need one for the ages," he said as he walked into the living room and took off his tank top. And then, as he did often since the release of *The Godfather* two years prior, he put some cotton in his cheeks, messed his hair, and did his best impersonation of Brando crying to the film's mortician Bonasera. "I need you to use all your skills and powers—"

"Daddy, stop," NuNu said. "You look too weird."

And then he was upon us, standing above the chair, wearing just his terry cloth shorts. He looked down, rubbed his belly, and yelled, "My body! Look how they massacred my body!"

He would fall into his chair and pretend to be passed out while we went and gathered the different lotions and oils to spread all over his body. Over the years, we used perfumed lotions and all sorts of body moisturizers. But in the last year or so—with my father complaining that parts of his body ended up unexpectedly itching him like crazy, we had to experiment with different oils and elixirs. What he said felt best was the tiniest bit of extra-virgin olive oil and a little elbow grease applied by the bunch of us. He would happily moan and groan like a big old giant in that chair. We would delicately apply it to his face and go all the way down to between his toes—two of which no longer had the ability to bend anymore.

"Dad," I said, "how can you not remember when your toes stopped bending?"

"I can't. I have no idea," he said. "Besides, toes are over-rated. They serve no purpose."

"They keep our balance," Gino said. "If we didn't have toes, we'd fall forward."

"Yeah," I said. "That makes sense. They keep us from falling on our face."

My father just smirked, put his hands up to momentarily stop the massage, and threw his logic on the fire.

"There are no toes on our heels," he said. "So why don't we fall on our asses every day?"

5

SPIDERS AND SNAKES

Mondays in the summertime held all the excitement of a wake. With a noisy, wonderful weekend behind us, it was always dreadful thinking I'd have to wait another five whole days before it could all begin again. Even though it was summer vacation and, at a whistle's notice, there could be twenty friends at my front door, I still woke up with a heavy heart. Mondays always seemed cruel to me, as so much of my family had to return to work their 9-to-5s. I would have absolutely no pep in my step. And that particular Monday morning, the first with Gino in our house, I was in those precious moments of the previous night's deep sleep slowly becoming the reality of a new day. I turned over to see Gino passed out in his cot next to my bed, some slobber running from his lips, his mouth wide open.

I stared at his face for some time, even squinting to give him the benefit of the doubt. But the verdict was in: he didn't even really, *truly* look like a Benza. And that puzzled me. We were a dark-skinned bunch. We didn't burn red from too much sun. We got brown. We weren't pudgy in any way like Gino was. We were more lean and mean. We had thick, straight, dark hair. We were lanky, despite the fact that we ate whether we were sitting down for dinner, lying down on the couch, or standing at the kitchen sink. We had long arms, tight stomachs, and legs that slightly bowed a bit. When I stared at Gino, he was shorter, softer, and a different shade of pale. And then the reality of what lay ahead hit me with the reality and speed of a Scorsese smash cut. I took it all in for a moment: I had finally noticed there was a pile of luggage in my small room. There were different clothes laid out on my chair. A toothbrush and a comb and deodorant that weren't mine. My room even smelled differently. Not bad or vile. Just the way your room smells when someone else has been breathing, yawning, farting, and coughing in it all night long. But instead of pulling my hair out in aggravation, I decided to have some fun. I put my bare feet within inches of Gino's nose for a few seconds, wiggling them wildly in the hopes I'd spring loose some horrible odor. Maybe a tiny bit of the bay was buried deep inside a toenail or two. When that didn't work, I balled up tiny bits of tissue and tossed them at his face, trying to get one in his mouth.

"And now Clyde Frazier works the ball up court, with the New

York Knickerbockers trailing by one to the Los Angeles Lakers," I whispered to myself. *"Six seconds on the clock in game seven as Frazier glides by Jerry West at midcourt and finds Earl 'the Pearl' Monroe coming off a high screen from Willis Reed. Monroe, moving left, lets loose a double pump, fadeaway from fifteen feet out. And he . . . sinks it. The Knicks have done it again. And the Garden floor is covered with New Yorkers. The Knicks are champions. And my ears can't believe what my eyes just saw!"*

After I had played out a few more far-flung fantasies and it didn't wake him up, I could hear the rumblings of my mother and father getting ready to go downstairs for coffee, so I cut to the quick. I got within an inch or so of his face.

"You *up*?"

"Wha-wha . . . ?"

"You look shot, man. You look like *you* drank all the wine last night," I said.

"I don't know." He yawned. "I guess the whole weekend caught up with me."

"Well, now it's fuckin' Monday. And I hate them."

Gino sat up in his cot. "What goes on around here during the week?"

Before I could even get a word out, my father burst into the room, rattling a wooden spoon inside a pasta pot. *"Drop your cocks and grab your socks!* We got work to do on the lower deck, sailors."

I had been a part of this staged, early-morning mayhem for years, so I was accustomed to watching my bedroom door fly open with various commands shouted from my father. I know for a fact, after spending some weekend mornings at my uncle's house in Jersey, that that little bit of my father's Monday-morning madness was more than I ever saw at my uncle's house. And that's no knock on my uncle or how he raised his family. It's just, as much as my father and uncle were basically the same men when they were together, they steered their families in different directions and at varying speeds when they were apart. I mean, if there was a volume knob on our houses, Uncle Larry's was on low. While our house had all its speakers blown out.

My father disappeared as quickly as he came in, but he continued to bang the spoon in the pot all the way down the stairs, singing reveille.

> I can't get 'em up; I can't get 'em up; I can't get 'em
> up this morning.
> I can't get 'em up; I can't get 'em up; I can't get 'em
> up at all!
> The corporal's worse than the privates; the sergeant's
> worse than the corporals.
> Lieutenant's worse than the sergeants, and the
> captain's worst of all!

My father always told me from his cherished days in the service that reveille was often followed by a canon shot. Since there was no canon on our front lawn, my father usually substituted that with a ferocious fart at the foot of the stairs. He could do them on queue.

Gino sat at the edge of the cot looking like an innocent man facing a sit-down with Old Sparky. "I don't think I can do this."

"Just get rid of that little hard-on, pull up some shorts, and follow me downstairs," I said. "You'll live."

Gino giggled like a girl. He half covered his lower self with a sheet. "What are you talking about?"

"Knock down that teepee," I said. "I *can see it*. Just hurry up and let's go. He don't like waiting."

"But I really should pee."

"Just hold it. Jesus, how much could that little pud hold? Come on."

Before we even got to the head of the stairwell, I was high off my father's scent of Winstons, Dentyne, and Old Spice cologne that still hung in my room. That was always enough to scurry down to the carpeted thirteen steps and meet him in the foyer. Gino arrived behind me, a bit disheveled, some fifteen seconds later. Two troops ready for duty.

My father stood at attention and tried with a straight face to apologize for the fart fog we were standing in. "I think your aunt Lilly snuck a little too much ricotta into the sauce last night and as a result, here we are. It'll pass."

He handed us each a *scolapasta* to head into the garden and pull from its bounty. Even though it was early in the morning, there was already a thick humidity outside, as we walked through the giant tomato plants and the zucchini and eggplant vines that were higher than our shoulders. My father would shout out into the thickness, "A.J., show Gino what to pick. I see an *abundanza* (abundance) in there."

I had to take Gino's glasses off his face before we got any further and clear the fog off them. "Okay, you can't work like this. So here's what we do," I said. "Pick any red tomato off the vine. But also grab any small ones that fell to the ground that aren't too dirty. Those are good for tonight's salad."

"I'm not really a lover of salad," Gino said.

"Lover of salad? Listen, that doesn't mean shit out here," I whispered. "Look . . . I ain't crazy about zucchini, but I still pick it. I just make the old man happy."

"Okay, okay."

"All right," I said. "Next thing you do is pluck any green pepper that's a little longer than your hand."

"Got it," he said, his eyes wandering like he fell down the rabbit hole with Alice. "What about these beautiful yellow flowers?"

"Hell yeah. Throw 'em in the pot. Those are zucchini flowers, and my mother fries them up in a batter and people go crazy for 'em. They're like some delicacy or something."

"Ahhh, they're so beautiful. Can't we just let them grow?"

Gino was in awe of being lost in all that vegetation. It looked like he felt more himself with not being seen or something.

"Uncle Al," he cried out. "Can't we just let the zucchini flowers grow and not eat them? They look so beautiful."

"I'm gonna make believe I didn't hear that," he said.

"Believe me, they look just as pretty frying in the pan."

"I don't know if I can do it," he said.

"This isn't up for debate, Gino," I said. "First you couldn't grab the clams and now you don't wanna pick the flowers? We *only* grow them so that we can pick them and eat them. End of story."

My father shouted into the garden. "Let's go. I got five minutes before I gotta go to work. I still see a lot more stuff—basil, mint, scallions. Come on, double-time it."

"All right, fuck it," I said. "I'll pick the goddamn zucchini flowers. But you better make sure you nail every tomato and pepper and eggplant."

Gino seemed somewhat content with that arrangement.

"But watch where you step," I said. "A strawberry patch is one thing. A pile of dog shit can change your whole day."

Lucky for me, there was a family of five girls and one boy living right next door to us. And on most mornings—with my father shouting instructions—it was almost a guarantee that my thirteen-year-old neighbor, Debbie Rossitto, would be at her bedroom screen window and overlooking everything we did. Whatever I said, or whatever I did, I always felt her presence peering down on me. And Debbie was far advanced for her age, at least physically and mentally. We shared a birthday—June 2—and she'd already told me she wanted me to be the one to take her virginity next summer. So, you can imagine, every move I made—every command I shouted out—I did so under the pretense that Debbie was listening and watching everything.

That would've been too much of a load for Gino to carry, so Debbie and I kept our flirting under control until those nights when we graduated to flashlight tag.

Like most days in the garden, on this particular morning, I saw Debbie move her curtain aside and watch us work. Seeing her pretty face while she slowly combed her hair and imagining her promise made gardening almost impossible. It's hard to look gorgeous through a screen window. The only girl I ever saw do that was Faye Dunaway in *Bonnie and Clyde*.

"A.J., what are you doing?" my father said, snapping me back. "There are at least six or seven tomatoes you walked right by. Come on, now, let's get this done. I gotta go sell carpet."

Somehow, I cleared my head and went back to grab the fruit. The *scolapasta* would be full, and that would make my father happy and send him off to work feeling good and whistling. With me not riding Gino's ass so hard, I could tell my cousin was feeling a little better about himself, and that allowed me to let my mind wander back to Debbie, my very own Bonnie Parker.

But there was one more thing my father had on his agenda: we had bugs, slugs, and worms to deal with. After giving us those detailed instructions, we followed him to his car, along with my mother right by our side. He hopped into his convertible instead of opening the door.

"Is that all you got for us today, Dad?"

"No. Three more things," he said, lighting a cigarette. "Be loud. Be boys. And break your mother's balls."

He screeched out of the driveway, drowning out my mother's reply, "*Up yours, Al Benza!*"

Beep. Beep.

And that was the last we'd see of him until around 10:00 p.m.

"Don't worry, Aunt Lilly," Gino said. "I'm not going to do that."

"Thank you, sweetheart."

"Do what?" I said. "Do what?"

"You know . . ." Gino replied. "What Uncle Al told us to do. At the end there."

My mother didn't like where this was going. It was mostly innocent, but I think she could see a little bit of the instigator I obviously inherited from my father. "Come on," she said. "Go back by the pool."

"No, not yet. I wanna hear Gino say what Daddy said."

"But . . . A.J.," Gino said, sheepishly looking up at my mom.

"Just say it. It ain't no big deal. Say, 'Break Aunt Lilly's balls.'"

"A.J., stop it," she said, now with a little force in her voice. "It's a figure of speech. *He* was breaking balls."

"See! You can say it, and Gino can't. Just say it and I won't bother you anymore about it."

Gino was silent for a few moments, I thought because he was forming the words. "Why are you throwing a conniption fit over this?" he said.

"Yeah, he's right," my mother warned. "Now knock it off before I crack a wooden spoon over your head."

"It's just a funny thing to say," I said, turning away for the backyard. "That's the way we talk around here, Gino. You better get used to it."

My mother messed Gino's hair and lightly pinched his cheek. "Don't get all worked up, honey. Sometimes he's too much like his father—who's the biggest ball-breaker of them all."

They laughed and lagged twenty feet behind me, and frankly, the possibility of having any passing friend see my cousin, along with my mother's horrifying muumuu—which hung from the shoulder with its brilliantly colored floral Polynesian patterns—was too much for me to take.

"Come on," I yelled. "You wanna see a conniption? We got slugs to kill!"

As beautiful as my father's garden was, there were infiltrators that we had to deal with. And my father didn't like to use any chemical sprays from the hardware store. He never trusted what that might do to his fruit or vegetables. Instead, he preferred we take matters in our own hands. But that tactic took an eagle eye, a strong stomach, and a memory without consideration for all God's creatures.

Finding the dreaded green tomato hornworm was the

equivalent of finding Waldo—thirteen years before the game was ever invented. The hornworm worked at night, devouring tomato, eggplant, and pepper plants. You had to wake up really early and look really closely to see them clinging to the underside of a branch near the trunks of the plants. They were almost impossible to spot because of their ability to camouflage so perfectly. And they were ugly and medieval-looking, with a bunch of little legs and a brown horn at one end of their thick three-inch body. Whenever we spotted one, our job was to pull it off the branch with a pair of pliers and drop it into a Maxwell House Coffee can of water and watch it drown. And these tough caterpillars—which, if they weren't caught, would become the five-spotted hawk moth—put up one hell of a fight.

I told Gino in no uncertain terms, "I'll go in there and pluck them. You just hold the coffee can. But if they start crawling out of the can, you gotta take a stick and shove them back in."

Why we didn't step on them and get it over with, I have no idea.

My father's instructions to kill garden slugs was even more sinister. We were to find the slimy critters—with or without their shells—and resort to a different type of torture: lightly sprinkle table salt on them and watch as they squirmed and dissolved to death like the Wicked Witch of the West. After our murderous run—with a canister of Morton Salt—Gino had had enough.

"Why can't we just step on them or hit them or throw them in the canal?" he said with genuine concern.

"I think my father wants any other slugs with the same idea to get the message," I said.

"It's like *The Godfather* in your garden," Gino said.

"Goddamn right," I said. "But it works, don't it?"

6

HOOKED ON A FEELING

Between the slicing and the dicing and the torturous melting of numerous insects in our garden, I had one more job I had to lay on Gino to see if he could pass some muster. It wasn't anything too nasty, but it did take place in the dark of night, and that could've easily made him mess his pants.

For as long as I could remember, we always caught our own night crawlers for weekend fishing trips. My father's reasoning was something on the level of "Whose fuckin' earth could produce better worms than the ones that crawl in our own backyard?"

And he was right. But how he was able to gather them was genius to a twelve-year-old. He would steadily bring home small scatter rugs from the store every few nights or so and carefully place them on the grass behind the homemade wooden cabana he had built with Frankie and Jack. Between that and the behemoth of a garden compost (a full forty years ahead of the Green Movement) *and* a large carob tree, whose pods were the molted remains of hundreds of cicada, it was like a Bermuda Triangle of darkness that nobody wanted to walk through when the sun went down. But with my father's orders to persistently water that particular area for an hour each night after dinner, what we would uncover was the kind of bounty that could keep a bait shop in business for months. See, by flooding that part of the yard with water and letting the carpet remnants get soaked, my father was mercilessly drawing the night crawlers to the damp, dark, and dank confines beneath the rugs. It didn't matter that the screaming army of cicadas were falling on the ground all around us. All Gino and I had to do was have one of us lift the rug, while holding a small flashlight in our mouths, while the other dived in with both hands and successfully kept the worms from disappearing back into their holes in a split second. I'd been on the physical end of this practice a hundred times. I wanted Gino to do the handiwork this time out. And that made for a long night.

It was close to nine, and I really wanted to show my father that I could persuade Gino to get down and dirty with the worms. But it wasn't looking good. For starters, we heard a frog croaking somewhere nearby, so that made the mood more tense than usual.

"What's that?" he said, clutching my sleeve.

"It's a frog. Don't worry about it. They don't bite and they're more scared of us than we are of them."

What's more, Gino had a hard time stepping on the squishy carpets in the dimly lit area behind the cabana.

"It feels like I'm stepping on bologna," Gino said. "Can't we wait until morning? I swear I'll get up early—"

"Shhh, man! These worms only come out at night. They're like vampires."

"Oh God," he said, holding a bucket of dirt. "This whole area, A.J. I feel like we're in that scary silent film. I swear Dr. Caligari is going to come out any second."

That gave me chicken skin. "Don't even *joke* about that movie," I said. "That gives me the willies."

Gino was taken aback. "Oh my God, something gives *you* the willies? I didn't think anything spooked you."

"Oh, I got my things that scare me shitless. Trust me."

"Tell me," Gino said.

"Nah, it's stupid. Come on. We gotta get worms."

"*I'm* scared of clowns," Gino volunteered.

That amused me, but I wanted to know more. "Clowns, huh? Clowns like Bozo? Like Ronald McDonald?"

"Nooo, not Bozo," he said. "And I'm pretty sure Ronald McDonald isn't a clown."

"Of course he's a clown," I said. "He's got the red nose, the crazy hair, the big shoes. What else does he have to do to prove to you he's a clown? What do you think he is? Seriously."

"I don't know. I never really thought hard about it. Just a guy who sells hamburgers, I guess," Gino said.

I let a minute or two pass before I said anything. "Hamburger salesman, huh?"

"I guess you're right," he said. "Now that I think of it."

I lifted a wet rug to see a half dozen or so really lazy earthworms. "Hold the light," I said. "I got these suckers!"

Despite the hard, quick work in front of us, Gino needed to be heard. I half looked for worms, and quickly scooped some up, while I waited for a response, any response, from him.

"I guess I'm scared of, you know, like the clowns people paint in pictures," he said. "Like sad clowns and stuff. Like the oil paintings of clowns that are in my basement."

"Yeah, well, you know what my father says?"

"I get the feeling it isn't good."

"My father says the clowns that show up at kids' parties are the kind of guys you should stay away from."

Gino thought for a moment, moving the worms around the can with a stick. "What do *you* think?"

I gave the dark yard a quick scan. "I think we need to lift four more rugs."

"No," he said. "What do you think about guys who dress up as clowns?"

"I think makeup is for girls, Gino," I said. "Not for old men chasing after kids and making balloon animals."

Gino stayed quiet and skittishly lifted a soaked shag rug while I quickly grabbed a dirty dozen caught half out of their holes. We methodically repeated this process a couple more times as our teamwork began to click. When we came to the last rug it felt like it weighed 100 pounds. It took both of us to break the rug's suction from the mud.

"Holy shit! The mother lode," I screamed. I held the flashlight in my left hand and went picking like crazy with my right. There were dozens of them all fat and happy that had squirmed too far from their holes. Even Gino grabbed a few and dropped them in the can really quick before wiping his hands on his shorts.

"Feels good, right?" I said.

"Yeah, I guess."

"Okay, one last rug," I said. "The one right by the compost. That's gonna be a tough one because we buried the fluke heads there on Saturday, remember?"

"Of course I remember. I'll never forget that for as long as I live."

"Okay, it's gonna stink like crazy. I've done this alone a million times. Just take short, quick breaths."

"Wait . . . should I breathe through my nose?" Gino said.

"Well, that just might make you wanna puke," I said. "And it'll take days before it leaves your sinuses."

"So then I should breathe through my *mouth*?"

"No. Then it'll feel like you ate them."

"Okay . . . so breathe through what hole, then?"

"Just breathe through both. A little at a time. You're not gonna die."

As we made our way over to the farthest corner of the yard, toward the croaking frog and nearer the stink, Gino piped up. "You never told me what *you're* scared of."

"*Now* you wanna talk about this?"

"It gets my mind off the odor."

"Fine. Okay. Definitely Dr. Caligari," I said through shorts bursts of little breaths. "And, uh, Dobermans. Yeah, there are these two Dobermans that live in a house at the end of the canal. And whenever we drive the boat by they go berserk. The crazy owner named 'em Dead and Gone. You imagine that?"

"That sounds horrifying," he said. "And those poor dogs have no idea what their names mean."

"I don't know, but the hell with that. This guy, he's a real asshole. Sometimes when he sees our boat coming and he thinks we're too close to his dock, he unchains them and they tear ass to the edge of the dock, barking and howling, with their feet kicking up rocks into the canal. Scary as all hell, man. It's like they want to jump in the boat and attack all of us."

"What's something else that scares you?"

"Ummm . . . besides the toes that don't bend on my father's feet?"

"No, really." Gino laughed. "Come on. Tell me."

I downshifted the tone real quick. "It's scary. It's pretty damn scary to *me* anyway. And you might be too young to hear it," I said. "If I tell you—do me a favor: I don't need you trying to climb into my bed and get under the covers with me tonight."

"Yeah, as if . . ."

"All right, I'm gonna tell you," I said quietly. "But don't get all crazy on me out here in the dark. We're in the farthest, most stinky and scary corner of the yard. Gino, I'm warning you. This could keep you up all night."

"As long as it isn't about clowns," he said.

"Okay," I began. "I don't like Dr. Caligari, Dobermans, and—ready?—dolls with wooden teeth and busted eyeballs. You happy now?"

With that, Gino dropped the bucket of worms, scampered across the damp scatter rugs, and shrieked into the house. *"Oh my GOD! Wooden dolls . . . broken teeth . . . lazy eyes! Who thinks of that?! Who thinks of that?!"*

Remember, he was reacting to things that scared *me*.

It took me twenty minutes to get him settled and calm by slamming a package of Drake's cupcakes on the table in front of him. "Listen to me . . . just eat these," I said. "I don't know why, but they'll make you feel better and calm you down."

"I'm not allowed to eat sweets like this," Gino said, rocking back and forth in his chair. "I'm not allowed."

I looked at this poor kid, staring at a cupcake like he was holding the losing hand in a million-dollar, high-stakes poker game. "Jeez, it's just a little old cupcake. What's the worst that could happen? Take a bite and see if you change at all."

Gino examined the Drake's cupcake like it was a lost artifact.

"I don't know . . ." he said. "I just see my mother and father telling me *not* to eat it."

"Wanna know the way I see it?"

"Okay," he said.

"My father woke us up at the crack of dawn's ass," I reasoned. "We spent a lot of time in the hot garden, picking fruit and vegetables and dodging dog shit and mosquitoes the whole time. And then we spent the last hour in pitch-black digging out worms, while dodging toads, cicadas, and God knows whatever-the-hell else, just so we can have a pleasurable fishing trip this weekend."

"Yeah, that is true," Gino said.

"You're goddamn right it's true. And it was hard and scary. Do I have to even remind you of you running away at the mention of dolls with wooden teeth and busted eyeballs?"

"Okay," Gino said, covering his eyes and squirming in the big wrought-iron kitchen chair. "Please don't bring that up again."

"But old wooden doll teeth and crazy eyeballs is something that scares *me*, not you," I said.

"I never thought of them before, and now they terrify me."

"Well, if you ask me, I say you *earned* that cupcake," I said.

Even in his panic, I managed to pick up the bucket of worms he dropped and scoop all of the escapees back inside.

And I brought that bounty into the house and showed my father, who was deep in the cold cut drawer, looking to make a sandwich.

"Dad, there's gotta be fifty worms in here," I said. "And more than a few 'bull-greezers,'" which was our word for anything or anyone that was bigger than the norm.

My father took a good, hard look at the can. "You think this is a good haul?" he said.

I looked at the amount of Scotch in his glass. It was at least three fingers high, and I knew that couldn't have been his first, since he'd been home from work for a while. Over the years, I learned those type of open-ended conversations could go both ways: splendid or scary. Happily or horrifyingly.

He picked up the Maxwell House Coffee can full of muddy dirt and filthy worms and calmly dumped the can on top of the Formica kitchen table. My mother, who somehow always managed to stay nearby at pivotal moments, piped up.

"Oh Jesus Christ, Al. Now all that shit is on the table we eat on," she carefully said. "What are you looking to do? Is there something you want to tell the kids?"

"Yeah, Lilly, there is something I want to tell the kids for your friggin' information."

"Here we go," my mother began, as Gino's anxiety—which he wore on his cute little face—began to appear.

"I *want* to tell my son and my nephew—while they scrounged around the yard—that what they did was . . . *fuckin'* beautiful. *Okay?* They got the mother lode of worms here. You know what this costs at a bait shop? Do you know, boys?"

"No, Daddy," I said, somewhat relieved. "How much?"

"I have no idea, because I don't sell fuckin' worms for a living." He laughed, a bit too loudly. "But I can tell you worked hard and you found a shitload of worms and there's no telling how many fish we'll catch with the worms you have here. I'll tell you one thing: we don't have to go to Augie's Bait and Tackle this weekend."

"Okay," my mother said, trying to mop up the emotions. "A.J., can you put the worms and the dirt back in the can?"

"I got it, Ma."

My father—most likely trying to turn his brother's desperate phone call into positive results—hugged and kissed me and Gino before elaborating on how important the worms were to helping us put food on our table. "A.J., *you've* done this before. But, Gino . . . having never done this . . . I gotta say I'm very impressed."

"Thanks, Uncle Al," Gino said, picking at his cupcake.

"Were you ever scared at all, with the unknowns of the backyard?"

"No," I said. "He was great, Dad. He got right in there."

"Beautiful," he said. "So, Gino, you had a good time?"

"Yes," he said. "It was different. It was a little scary. But, I got the hang of it. It was fun."

"Good," my father said. "Tomorrow morning I'm gonna make you feel even better at o-seven-hundred hours."

"Wait, what?" I said. "We did good. Can't we sleep in tomorrow?"

"It's not all about you," my father said. "This is for Gino. You wanna feel better every day?" he asked Gino.

"Well . . . yeah."

"Do you trust your uncle Al?"

"Of course."

"Then I'll see you guys before I go to work in the morning."

"It can't wait until tomorrow night?" I asked.

"No. And hey . . . do me a favor. Clean the table. There are worms all over the place. Make your mother happy."

7

RADAR LOVE

My mother was nice enough to gently walk into my room and shake Gino and me awake a few minutes before 7:00 a.m. Neither one of us particularly cared that she had made some potato and eggs for us, but if she hadn't woken us up, we would have probably suffered through the indignity of another reveille and canon shot from my father. So we got up, pulled on some shorts, and headed down to the kitchen. My father was seated there, dressed sharply for work and all, reading the paper and grimacing through a cup of what my own mother always admitted was the "worst coffee ever made."

We sat at the table with the potato and eggs too steaming hot to eat, while we rubbed the sleep from our eyes. Gino and I stared at each other—but didn't dare say anything—as we readied for this gigantically important moment my dad promised us the night before.

As usual, he was reading the obituary section first. "Let me see here," he said real low. "Aaron . . . Abelson . . . Addison . . . Allen . . . Aponte . . . a lot of As checked out. Almost all in their sleep. Lucky bastards."

"Are those all dead people?" Gino asked me.

"Yeah. He reads this section expecting to find his name."

Gino twisted his face in confusion. "What?"

"Boys, eat," my mother said. "It's gonna get cold."

My father went on with the names of the dead. "Baker . . . Battaglia—I think I sold him carpet. Bay . . . Beale . . . Getting closer," he said. "Behrens . . . Bellini . . . Bent . . . ah, shit, Bittinger. Nope. Not there yet," he said aloud. "Your *friend* up there passed me by again."

He folded the paper away and got back to his last gulp of bad coffee.

"Why do you check the death notices, Uncle Al?" Gino asked.

"If I told you, you wouldn't believe me—like the rest of my family," he said.

Gino mounted up as much courage as he could. "Umm . . . why don't you try me?"

My father checked his wristwatch, knowing he could give Gino only the CliffsNotes version of his weekly nightmare/comedy bit. We had heard it a hundred times already.

It was brand-new territory for Gino.

"Maybe you've seen the funeral parlor down the street," my father began. "It's called Chapey's. And I have dreams that the owner of the funeral home, Fred Chapey, he tosses rocks at my window to wake me up, see? "

"Let me take it from here, Dad," I said. I knew it by heart. "And in that shadow hour before dawn, his rocks at the window wake you up and he says real scary-like, 'Al . . . .we need you. When are you coming up the street? Business is dead.'"

"That's terrible," Gino said.

"Did I get it right, Dad? What did I miss?"

My father turned his empty coffee cup and laughed at the pile of bitter grinds at the bottom. "You forgot that he's standing at the foot of the driveway and he's holding a brand-new black suit that I'd be buried in. He's holding a suit because I don't own one."

"Ew . . . that gives me chills," Gino said.

My mother, as usual, stepped in to break up the calamity. "Jesus Christ, what are you filling these kids' heads with? Don't make your dreams become their nightmares, Al."

"You didn't hear the rocks on the window?"

"I couldn't hear a hurricane over your snoring."

"That's great, Dad," I said, "but we woke up at seven—and this is my summer vacation—because you had something very important to do with us. Can we get to the point here?"

My father reached into his jacket pocket and fished out a plastic bag of pills. He tossed them on the table toward Gino.

Gino seemed a little alarmed, but not too much because he was very familiar with the pills inside the bag. I guess he was embarrassed a bit because we were all present.

My father spoke up. "Now, I'm no doctor—but I *am* an ex-undercover narc—and it looks to me like there are about one thousand pills, vitamins, and supplements in this here bag," he said. "Your father told me to make sure you keep up with this regimen while you are here with us. You know about this, right?"

"Yes, Uncle Al," he said. "Those are the medicines I have always taken every morning that will eventually make me feel better . . . and better."

"Better and *better*," my father repeated.

"Yeah, that's the plan," Gino said, finally eating his potato and eggs.

"What does the term *better and better* mean to you?" my father asked.

Gino put his fork down, twirled his hair with his left hand, and tried to answer the question. "I guess . . . you know . . . that the longer I take the medications, the more I will get better and better."

"Better and better," my father said, with little emotion—weighing the bag of pills in his hand. "Is this a phrase you and your father say a lot?"

"Well, yeah," Gino said. "It's part of the mind-control meetings my father goes to."

My mother and father exchanged looks like I'd never seen

before. Like they had both just seen a UFO. He pulled her away from the table.

"Take the kids out by the pool," my father told my mother. "Do something with them. Use your imagination. I gotta call my brother right now."

I remember my father rushed to the phone like he was on a mission. I don't recall the term *better and better* sounding too weird to me, but when Gino mentioned mind control, my throat got a little tight. Somehow I just knew it was tied to the bumper sticker my uncle Larry always had on the back of his many sports cars. Each time he visited with a new car it always seemed like he would replace the I'M OK—YOU'RE OK bumper sticker. I only remember that decal because I can't ever forget my father's disdain and confusion over people who needed to get a message to you through the use of their cars. And I especially remember the uproar that started the day my uncle gushed about the self-help book of the same name a couple of summers earlier. To Uncle Larry, the pioneering work of a brain surgeon in uncovering the neurological basis of memory that could offer complementary insights grounded in reality was something divine. Looking back now, maybe it was something he thought could make sense of what was happening to the boys in his family. To my father, it was all a bunch of nonsense—and I remember him saying it was even worse that so many millions of people were reading the book and buying into it. "But Al," Uncle Larry said, "it's just a bumper sticker."

To which my father replied with a snicker. "A bumper sticker isn't a method of solving problems in life, Larry," he said. "I got a better sticker, Larry. 'I'm OK, the author is a shithead.'"

Anyway, my mother, Gino, and I were outside, counting how many yellow jackets were working like crazy inside the grape arbor. We stopped counting at a hundred. But I could see my father through the screen window, talking to my uncle Larry with his hands. Like all Italians I'd been around, his hands filled in the spaces between the words. One shrug could equal a soliloquy. Two palms stuck together, pointing downward and moved up and down could end an opera.

"You wanna tell me about this 'mind control' shit, Larry?" my father said. "I got your kid here talking to me like he's brainwashed—forget brain *damaged*—and he's telling me this fuckin' bag of pills are going to make him 'better and better' or whatever the fuck."

Whatever Uncle Larry said on the phone was supposed to pacify my father. But it was now obvious to me that both of Gino's parents had gone to the ends of the earth to try and make him fit in. To basically try to "cure" him.

Uncle Larry had Gino on a daily cocktail of prescription drugs, vitamins, and supplements that numbered as many as twenty pills a day to reverse the "brain damage." Each morning he'd been with us, I'd watched Gino gag and almost puke attempting to swallow some of the larger pills.

"How do you do it?" I said to him. "Some of those are friggin' horse pills."

"It's gonna help in the long run," he said, holding a huge cup of tap water.

After the phone call between my father and Uncle Larry, a new regimen was prescribed. My father came out with a giant shopping bag filled with Gino's pills and dropped them on the ground by the back garden.

"Gino," he said. "These are the pills your father left for you to take—with specific instructions and all. For some reason he thinks these pills will make you feel better."

"I know," Gino said. "We've been doing it this way as long as I can remember."

"Well, let me ask you a question, how do you feel now?"

"I'm a little tired, but I feel fine, Uncle Al."

"If you ask me, Gino, this is all a *fizzeria*." (*Fizzeria* was my father's word for anything that he considered to be bullshit.) "You understand what I'm saying? Everything you need to live on is in *that* garden or in the bay or in what your aunt Lilly puts on the table for dinner."

"I'm sure you're right," Gino said.

"I'm not going to argue with you there."

"Then what are we going to do with all those pills?" Gino said.

"What do you want to us to do?" I said.

"I don't know what to say," he said. "It's hard to tell the truth sometimes, Uncle Al and Aunt Lilly."

"Gino, we're your family," my mother said. "You can tell your family anything."

"Well, *this* family is like that," he said. "That's for sure."

Gino's eyes filled with tears for a bit. I didn't bother asking him why. He would've blamed it on allergies again, probably.

"I guess I'm sick and tired of almost puking every morning taking these pills. And they really don't make me feel any different."

"I figured that," my father said. "That's why I got a second opinion with another doctor who feels the same as you."

"What doctor?" Gino asked.

"Another Dr. Benza," he said.

"What are the chances of that?"

"None," my father said, popping his bubble. "It's me. I'm in control of your medication now."

Gino laughed a little. "What do we do?"

My father told me to go and fetch the shovel behind the cabana. "Not the flat one," he said. "Get me the spade. You're gonna dig a hole."

I brought back the spade and watched my father point to a spot in the ground back by the part of our yard that was nearest the canal. "Dig a nice hole two or three feet deep," he said. I loved gardening work, so I was done in a minute or so.

"Gino," my father said. "Lemme see the big bag of bullshit medicine my brother has you taking."

Gino handed over the bag a bit sheepishly. "Here, Uncle Al."

"Okay," my father said. "Now then, you're gonna bury every single pill in this bag and it's my contention you'll feel fine from this day forward."

Gino tilted the bag and the pills poured out like shrimp from a basket. I pushed the earth over them and the pills disappeared within seconds, like dirt on a dead relative's casket.

"You won't tell my mom or dad, will you, Uncle Al?"

My father shook his head. "You bet your sweet bippy I won't." They kissed on it. And Gino never took a pill the rest of the summer.

8

THE BOYS ARE BACK IN TOWN

It didn't bother me, but it was obvious that my father had begun to relegate a certain part of his attention, his guard, and his heart toward Gino. Maybe it was something about that pill ceremony, but I think he could feel—well, we *all* could somewhat feel—that my cousin had different sorts of issues he was dealing with in his head and at his home in Jersey. Sometimes my father would tell Gino to pour him a Scotch and he would take me aside in the kitchen, all alone, and gently but firmly tell me to "keep an eye on your cousin." Or "this can't be easy for him . . . being away from home and all."

"I know, Dad, I will."

"And if you see any of your friends give him any bullshit,

you put an end to it right on the spot," he said. "You know how to take care of things. Otherwise, you bring me in."

"What kind of crap, Dad?"

"You know what I'm saying," he said, with a gleam in his eye. "If you see any one of these *testa di minghia* (pricks) saying anything to your cousin about being, you know, different and all . . . you let me know."

"Yeah, Dad. I got it."

He stood there by the sink, lifted up his shirt, and asked me scratch his back. I did so until my fingertips burned.

"Listen to me, we all got shit we gotta get through. Some things are visible; some aren't. I gotta be honest, Gino's problem is a tough nut to crack for me. But we're gonna get there. We gotta get there."

"Yeah, yeah," I said, as I raked his back until it slightly bled in spots.

"Okay, Okay, that's good. I love you. Kiss your poppa," he said, lowering his shirt."

And how I loved that.

As far as I can recall, that's as close as he ever flirted with telling me his feelings on why Gino was staying with us that summer. I don't think he felt I wasn't ready to hear it, I just think he didn't want to call too much attention to the cards Gino was dealt or the cards he was holding in his hand.

"Hey, Gino," he shouted. "Where's my Scotch? That's *my* nightcap, not yours."

"Coming . . . coming, Uncle Al."

"You're a good kid," he told him. "But a shitty bartender."

I faced a lot of pressure getting Gino accepted by my friends, let me tell you. Laughing and playing around with your family was one thing, but mixing him in with the boys on the block was another. Oftentimes cruel and ritualistic. I was constantly peppered with questions about him the first day I brought him out of the house. I felt like I had to make excuses for him before they had even met him. And it was all because there were a bunch of little problems that added up to a big issue. And—gun to my head—the issue was, he just didn't act the way the other boys did. Plain and simple, while agonizingly difficult to understand.

He couldn't throw a spiral. He couldn't hit a baseball or catch a grounder. He shot off the wrong foot at hoops. He couldn't dive into the pool. He wasn't very fast, so playing Rumbles or "kill the guy with the ball"—where a ball carrier ran around the field endlessly while every other guy took turns tackling him to the ground—was out of the question for him. Wrestling on the lawn wasn't an option. And there was absolutely no point in lifting weights in someone's garage. Chasing girls? He was only ten, and I just didn't see that as something that got his motor running.

The smirks and comparisons started slowly. Believe it or not, the fact that he was from Jersey was the first hurdle I faced in getting him mixed in with the bunch of boys I ran with.

"Jersey?" Richie Tischler said. "That whole state smells like rotten farts."

Back then, most of us responded to street whistles or hearing a few friends flat out yell your name in front of your house in the street. That was enough to drop whatever you were doing and start planning the day with twenty or so kids all within the same age range. We played stickball, stoopball, kick the can, leapfrog, softball, kickball, basketball, hard-pitch baseball, or tackle football. We even played flashlight tag at night and used about five of our neighbors' backyards to hide in, and not one neighbor complained. It all depended on how we felt at that particular point of the day. Majority ruled. Most days, we had so many kids showing up to play whatever sport we chose that we actually had to tell the stragglers who were a bit late to be picked for sides: "Sorry, game's locked." This meant you were "locked out" of playing. And people turned around and went home, knowing they had to show up earlier the next day if they wanted to be a part of the fun.

I carefully unveiled Gino, like a fragile ceramic, with not enough time in the forge. I folded him into games that might suit him best.

I suggested kickball to a gang of ten friends or so at my door, some riding Sting-Ray bikes, with baseball cards in the spokes that went *rat-a-tat-tat*—like Bobby DeRusso—who also had a banana seat and extended forks. His parents weren't rich or anything, but Bobby's father always made sure he bought the best version of everything, with all the new gadgets. And what really sucked was that Bobby would never let you take his bike for a spin. "Who's this?" Bobby said, sizing up Gino.

"This is Gino, my little cousin from Jersey. He's staying here for a few weeks."

"Yeah, huh?"

"I was thinking we could play a game of kickball across the street in the school yard," I said.

"Kickball? I don't think so," Bobby said, while popping a wheelie on my driveway. "There's a bunch of seventh-grade girls playing volleyball over at the Beach Fields. I say we go there and check 'em out. I saw Sue Annino there. And she ain't wearing a bra."

This whipped the other guys into a frenzy. Sue Annino was flat-out gorgeous and so out of reach even though we were the same age. On any other day, I would have crawled there to watch her play. I could have stared at her the whole day. I used to see her face in the moon at night, but nobody believed me. I knew that wasn't Gino's bag. I wrapped up the resentment bubbling in me and stuck to kickball. "Nah, I don't feel like walking a mile to the Beach Fields, man. And Sue wouldn't give us the time of day. I say we just roll the ball out and go five-on-five kickball."

"Suit yourself," Bobby said. "I'm gonna go see Annino's nips." When he raced off on his rear tire doing a wheelie, that left nine of us. So I volunteered Gino as the automatic pitcher. So we'd be playing four-on-four, with Gino pitching for both sides. All he had to do was roll the ball toward home plate and let the boys kick away. Least stressful job on the field.

I took Gino by the shirt and talked closely as I walked with him. "You ever play this game?"

"I think so," he said. "Um, in gym class."

"Okay, this is the same thing, only outside. Listen to me," I said quietly, "just roll the ball to the white T-shirt on the ground. If it's kicked to you and you catch it, you gotta throw it at the runner and he's out."

"Okay, I can do that," he nervously said.

"Trust me," I said. "No one ever kicks the ball to the pitcher. These guys can kick *far*. So I'll be right behind you in centerfield."

"Okay," Gino said. "But if you really wanna go see that girl, Sue or whatever, I could stay home with Aunt Lil and Aunt Mary. . . ."

"Nah. Another time."

Some of the guys took off their shirts to use as bases. I couldn't get mine off quick enough, that's why I was the brownest kid in the neighborhood. The whole summer felt like ninety degrees, and I soaked it up. I loved that feeling. No oil, no Coppertone, no nothing. Just sweat.

"Let's go. Pitch!" Richie Tischler yelled from behind the makeshift home plate.

"Cool your jets," I yelled back. "I'm getting my team together."

I covered everything kicked to centerfield and leftfield. Pete D'Ascoli, my next-door neighbor, who was as fast as a cougar, covered the other side of the outfield. David O'Keefe played between first and second base, and his older brother, Danny O'Keefe—who was fourteen—covered anything down the third-base line and whatever was kicked toward shortstop. Pete and I were quick and had great hands. The O'Keefe brothers were solid on the bases. But we all knew we had a lot of ground to cover with Gino pitching. It wasn't anything anyone said, but it just, sort of, hung in the air, like the heavy Long Island humidity.

"Jesus . . ." Perry Underhill yelled. "Can we freakin' start?"

"Suck my nuts, Pericles," I said. He was Greek. "All you do is pop it up to third. *Every* single time."

"You wanna bet?"

"Bet!"

"Okay. If I hit a homer, you gotta come over here and kiss my ass."

"All right," I said. "How 'bout if you don't, I get to kiss your hot sister Elenie's ass?"

"That's it," he huffed. "Giro, roll the ball."

"It's Gino," my cousin said softly. "But it's okay . . ."

"Gino . . . *Beano*. Whatever the hell it is, just roll it!"

"Take it easy," I yelled. Gino turned around and gave me a tense look. And I gave him a nod of encouragement.

"Keep it to the left side of the shirt," I said to him. "We got your back."

It took about a dozen pitches before Gino got anywhere near the plate. And the boys on the other team were losing their patience, and before long the dreaded chant started:

"We want a new pitcher, not just a belly itcher!" And on and on, with each pitch. This was destroying whatever ounce of confidence Gino might have even mustered up.

I called a time-out. And we all converged around Gino.

"What's wrong?" I asked him. "All you gotta do is roll the ball in an area so that these assholes can kick it."

"I know," he muttered. "I was doing pretty good I thought . . ."

"Nah . . ." Pete said. "You're nowhere near the plate."

"Can we just frickin' play?" Again Tischler, the smart-ass, piped up, making it harder on Gino's concentration.

I tapped Gino on the cheek. "Look at me. Don't listen to him. *Or* the Greek," I said. "Just roll the ball straight to the shirt. Let them kick it. We got you. Right, guys?" And with that my buddies gave an unenthusiastic reply. "Yeah. Right. Just let 'em kick it. Fuck these dicks."

We broke the team huddle and went back to our positions.

With Underhill digging in, about five feet behind the plate, Gino finally rolled a ball that was straight down the middle, but it hit a couple of small dirt mounds, so it had the potential to be a perfect offering for anyone lining up to kick the shit out of it. And Underhill did just that. *BOOM!* He laid into it, and I hadn't seen Perry do that in the thousand games we had played since we were each eight years old.

Perry managed to kick it off a slight bounce, so he had a lot of air underneath it, and it was headed somewhere in between Pete and me. And once those balls bounced once, it was over. It could've easily kept rolling another two hundred feet or so. But somehow Pete managed to get his hand on it and, magically, knock it over to me. At this point, Underhill—who wasn't terribly fast—was nearing second. I managed to grab the ball and—ignoring my cutoff man, Danny—came charging toward the infield with the ball in my right hand and Underhill almost at third.

A kiss on Elenie's ass was on the line here. I had to do something spectacular.

Danny was begging for me to pass him the ball, since Underhill was so close to him, but I charged to the infield with the ball held high above my head, ready to ding him before he reached home. I was several feet from Gino, and Underhill was getting ready to slide in for a home run, when I unleashed a perfect throw that was headed straight for his head a full ten feet before he would've scored.

"Slide! Slide! Slide, you Greek geek," Tischler screamed.

My throw was on line perfectly, leading the runner just by a few feet. And with no umpire, the "safe" or "out" call was going to come to a majority vote. With Underhill in full-slide mode and one or two feet from the plate, the big red ball slammed against his head right as he reached home.

"Yes! Fuckin' out, no doubt!" I yelled, with my teammates saying variations of the same. Obviously, Perry's team felt the opposite—that the ball hit him *after* his leg slid across the T-shirt.

When the dust literally cleared, we were all still arguing, while Gino stood on the pitcher's mound, not really knowing what to say or what to do.

Underhill and I were screaming at each other, but nothing was getting accomplished. "This has to go to vote," Tischler said. "The automatic pitcher has final say-so. It's up to Gino."

I don't think Gino had any idea of the weight of what lay in his hands at that moment. Not only was his pitch horribly easy to slam, but it also featured my running a good fifty yards with my heart pumping through my rib cage while making a perfect throw at Perry's long-haired, sweaty head.

"Okay, fine," I said. "Gino has final say. I'm cool with that." So, as we were huffing and puffing, I told Gino to make the call. "Was he safe or out, Gino? It's your call. Otherwise we'll be here all night and that was the first play of the game!"

Gino was sweating more than any of us, and all he had done was roll the damned ball. He looked around at all the players before he nervously made his call between a bunch of kids who had histories and rivalries and all sorts of stuff.

"I think the ball hit Perry's head . . . mostly his hair . . . umm . . . *after* he reached home."

Wait. What?

My cousin had ruled against me? I had rolled him out of the house, told him what to do and how to do it, and acted like his biggest bodyguard, and he ruled against me?

"Yes!" Underhill said, unbuttoning his cutoff dungarees and turning his white ass toward me. "Kiss my ass, Benza."

And, as disgusting as it sounds, a side bet is a side bet, and they are always to be honored. So I had to walk past Gino while stopping to say, "Ya know, he said, 'Kiss my ass, Benza,' and both our names are Benza. So this could easily be you kissing this dirtbag's ass."

"I'm so-sorry," Gino stammered. "I forgot about the bet."

"Well, that was *all* I was thinking about," I said.

With the whole field of guys laughing and catcalling, I mustered up the nerve to approach Underhill. "My father says Greeks and Turks don't wash a lot," I said. "When was the last time you washed your ass? I mean, *really* washed it? Like, scrubbed it."

"I don't know, what's today?" Underhill said. "Monday? Probably . . . April."

"You dick!" I said, before tripping him to the ground and grazing his butt with my lips before I punched his ass cheek as hard as I could.

"Oh, hurts so gooood," he said. "We're up, one–zip."

As I walked back to the outfield, Gino looked like he was about to pass out from the high stakes of a simple game of kickball.

"I'm sorry," he said. "I told you I would've stayed home so you could see that pretty girl."

"Gino . . ." I said, dripping exasperation as much as sweat. "Just roll the ball. How hard can that be?"

It wasn't hard at all. As a matter of fact, after thirty minutes or so my team hadn't even gotten up to kick yet and we were losing 11–0. When Ronnie Micelli finally popped up to David O'Keefe, we had recorded three outs and it was our turn to play offense. But in that half hour, Gino had had multiple chances to catch pop-ups (he didn't catch a one), throw runners out (he missed by a mile), and try to stop grounders up the middle (they knocked *him* over).

By the time he was rolling the ball to *my* team, he was gassed. I didn't think any ten-year-old kid, let alone a kid who'd rather be watching *Hodgepodge Lodge*, could last that long. So when Pete, the O'Keefe brothers, and I kept belting loooong home runs and tied the score at 11–11 in the first inning, it was time to stop the game, walk back to my house, and pick a new sport.

"This sucks," Tischler said. "Four-on-four doesn't work. Let's play Rumbles."

"I'm thirsty," Gino told me. "I'm gonna go inside and grab a Shasta."

"Okay," I said. "See you in a few minutes."

It was then when I got barraged with questions and the interrogation began.

"Dude . . ." Tischler said, sympathetically. "What's with this kid? He can't catch, he can't throw, he can't field a grounder if his life depended on it."

"Yeah, he had a tough game," I said. "I don't think they play kickball in Jersey or something."

"Nah, we're talking basic sports skills," Pete said. "He doesn't have them. I think we all knew how to throw a ball at five years old."

This got the guys laughing, and their bully train was leaving the station.

"Don't forget," I said. "The kid is ten. He doesn't play in any Little League sports or nothing. He's behind a little."

"*Dude*," Tischler chimed in. "He runs with his hands over his head. That's the way chicks run. It's like I'm watching my little sister, Regina, out there."

"We should set up a race between Gino and Regina to see who wins. . . ." Underhill laughed.

"Come on, come on," I said. "We're picking on him a little too much here. He doesn't know anyone, he's missing home, suddenly he's in a different house. He'll come around. The next game we play, I bet he'll be fine."

"I don't want him on my team, *whatever* the sport," Tischler said.

"Yeah, I gotta admit," Pete said. "I can't see him hitting a baseball. Can you imagine that? Or a tackle-football game?

The first time I send him out on a down-and-in, the ball's gonna hit his face before he can put his hands up."

"All right," I said. "I know what you mean, but I gotta work him in with us and you guys gotta help me. Whattya say?"

There was a silent gap in the conversation for a good fifteen seconds, almost like we knew the next person to speak up was gonna open a big can of worms. The consensus was hanging in the air, but no one had the nerve to reach up and pull it down and examine it.

"Hey . . ." Tischler said blankly. "You ever think you cousin might be a *fairy*?"

I have to admit that thought banged around my head a little before I had the guts or knowledge to address it. It bothered me only in the sense that it was bothering my friends. And that it was gonna mess up my summer. To me, it had no meaning beyond that. It was more an aggravation and an issue *I'd* have to deal with. I never really thought about what it represented to Gino.

"That would explain a lot, man," David O'Keefe said.

"I don't know," I said. "Can't be. His father is wild. I know *he* loves beautiful women and he played ball in high school, and I think he killed a bunch of krauts in World War II. I got the pictures to prove it. You should hear the stories he and my father tell!"

The boys, who were wiping the sweat off their bodies with their T-shirts, kind of let all that information sink in, right there in the thick air on my porch.

"But let's say he *is* a fairy. What's to stop a fairy from play-ing sports?" I said.

"It isn't about that. Do you know a fairy who *likes* to play sports?" Pete said. "They don't like sports, so they're not good at sports."

"So, we'll *make* him good at sports. Maybe this summer will change him," I said.

"I don't know," David O'Keefe said. "I don't think it can be done. Do you know any Major Leaguers or guys in the NFL who are queer *and* can play? Name one."

"So now what?" I said. "We don't hang out anymore this summer? I can't bring him around because he's not as good an athlete? That's fucked-up, guys."

As much as Perry Underhill could be a prick at times, he also possessed an understanding side on account of not having a father around, having kind of a crazy younger sister and an older heroin-addicted sister, Athena. Those were the things that he carried. And we never razzed him about those issues. So it wasn't too much of a surprise when he stepped off the bully pulpit and agreed we needed a plan.

"You know what?" he said. "We don't always have to make this about sports. We do stupid shit all the time. Maybe he'd like to see us blow up frogs with firecrackers? Or maybe do some ring-and-runs ya know, some prank phone calls . . ."

"I swear I'll ring Walter Modell's doorbell tonight," Tischler said, "and light a bag of dog shit on fire!"

"See, see," I said. "Now we're talking. This is good."

"You wanna throw all of Mr. Poland's lawn furniture into his pool tonight when he's sleeping?" O'Keefe said.

"Fuckin A. But let's start him out slow. This is gonna be fun, guys. And you'll be helping me a lot."

"I still say he's a Mary-ass," Tischler said. "And I don't think you can change a fairy once you've decided to become a fairy."

"All right, whatever," I said. "I'm not here to solve the problem, I just don't want him to feel awkward—being a *fem* or not being a *fem*."

The guys kind of just shrugged their shoulders and gave the plan a green light.

"You're the guy who's gotta sleep with him every night," Underhill said. "I'd keep one eye open."

"Oh, Christ," I said. "Hit the showers, Pericles. You still smell like last week's baklava."

And with that, the boys and I split up and went our separate ways. I wanted to dip in the pool, get the sweat off my body, and check in with Gino. I was actually trying to let all this new information settle in my brain. I even thought I could cut my father in on it, get his take on things.

My cousin a fairy? Benza boys didn't go that way, far as I knew. And what did it all actually mean anyhow, when you really think about it. I jumped in the pool and swam four whole laps underwater. I did my best thinking down there, which is to say I gave my brain a break from thinking much of anything. When I was done and drying off, I went upstairs to change. I passed by the bathroom and couldn't help but hear Gino crying. I stood there motionless by the door, annoying drops of water rolling down my legs, listening for clues as to why he suddenly split to go bawl his eyes out. I also noticed that he had taken the rotary phone into the bathroom with him. After a few minutes of me listening to his sobs, I slid the tip of my fingernail into the doorknob and quietly unlocked it. He was talking to someone on the phone, but I couldn't make out the words, on account that he left the faucet running. But the frustration and embarrassment was bubbling up within me. Busting in on him during such a private moment would have made me a downright prick of a cousin. That act was not what my Uncle Larry could've pictured in his mind as a place for his son to become a stronger boy and reverse the "brain damage." And it was certainly not what my father would have approved of.

But I did it anyhow.

Gino shrieked and immediately hung up the phone when I crashed into the bathroom. He was sitting on the john, with tears streaming down his face. He couldn't have been in a more prone position. But, instead of being a sweet, understanding, coddling cousin, I let free all the anger, frustration, and mystery that I'd been bottling up inside me.

"Who the hell were you talking to, and why are you crying?" I said as I slammed the door behind me.

"A.J., please just leave me alone. . . ."

"No. This is pissing me off," I said. "You didn't go inside for a Shasta. You went inside the house because you didn't want to play sports anymore with me and the guys."

He sat there on the bowl, quietly sobbing and wiping his tears with toilet paper.

"Can't I *just* be alone," he said.

"No. Gino, . . . I wanna know who you were talking to and what's making you cry. Jesus, the game ended in a tie!"

"But you know I'm not good at sports," he said. "And I was really bad at kickball today. Maybe you should just play with your friends without me."

At this point, I'd had it with his maudlin attitude, and I was determined to get him to change his ways, get stronger, and be more like me and the guys.

"Who were you talking to?" I said. "I'm not opening the door until you tell me."

"It was my mother, okay?" he said. "I just miss her and I wanted to see how she was doing. And she told me I don't have to do anything I don't want to do."

"What the hell does that mean?"

Gino started crying in his hands. "It means I don't enjoy the same stuff as you and your friends. And I don't have to play games I'm not good at. Kickball or diving or whatever . . ."

I don't know what came across me in the seconds after he finished his sentence. But I pounced on him, pulling him off the toilet bowl and wrestling him until his back was pinned to the cold, hard tile. "Just fuckin' do what I say, do what me and my friends do, and you'll be fine. You won't be calling home and crying to Mommy."

My mother yelled from the kitchen. "What the hell is going on up there?"

"Listen to me," I whispered. "Wash your face; make it look like you weren't crying for God's sake. You think this is easy on me?"

"What do you mean?" he said, somewhat composing himself.

"You know what I mean. Just fix yourself up and go watch TV," I said. "We're not playing any more sports today. All the guys went home, so don't worry about it."

"Well, don't be mad at me," he said as I opened the bath-room door.

"I ain't mad," I said. "I'm just . . . I don't know . . . confused. I don't get what you're crying over." I lingered in front of the mirror a few seconds. "Listen, I'm sorry I went apeshit there for a few seconds. I'm going back in the pool to think."

"Do you want to watch *The Electric Company* or *Zoom* or something?" he said.

"Yeah, but not right now," I said. "Lemme jump back in the pool. I'll see you in a little while."

"Okay . . . I'm sorry," he said.

"Gino, don't *apologize*," I said. "You didn't do anything wrong. Just cool your jets. We'll figure it out."

9

RIGHT PLACE, WRONG TIME

Don't think for a second I didn't swim my laps and flip around the deep end of my pool so that Debbie Rossitto couldn't see. I made it a point to make noise, hoping that she'd either appear at her bedroom window, or even better, come to the fence in her one-piece mesh bathing suit.

She had a wonderful mother but a *really* strict father, who wasn't home a lot, but when he was, that house of five girls and one boy became as quiet as a church. But when Daddy was gone, Debbie did her best to rouse me. After a fifteen-minute swim, I looked up from beneath the diving board to see her standing by the chain-link fence that separated our houses.

"What's up, *Rosey Toes?*"

"The Coogan brothers are in front of your house, you know that, right?" she said. "All three of them. Are you supposed to be doing something with them?"

Debbie was like the neighborhood's mayor.

"The Coogans?" I said. "Nah. I didn't call for them today. Danny's cool. His brothers are numb nuts though."

"Well, they're just standing there on the sidewalk, doing nothing," she said. "But I never trust that family."

I waved her over. She was wearing that mesh swimsuit I liked. "Forget about those guys."

"Whatcha doing?" she said.

"Just hanging out for a while," I said, making sure my hair was just right.

"I'm coming over. You wanna hang out in the raft for a while?"

"Yeah," I said. "The raft, it's right here. Come on in. The water is eighty degrees."

When she stepped down into the pool, I knew her prophecy would come true. But we were still a year away, which made the tension as tight as a snare drum.

Debbie was developed enough that the drop in the pool temperature was enough to give her chicken skin and, more important, to awake both nipples to stand out and completely knock out my peripheral vision.

She climbed in and snuggled next to me in the raft, both of us giggling about the probability of falling over.

When the water stopped churning and we regained our

balance, all I cared about was that she smelled of Bazooka bubble gum and Coppertone. And that made me forget about every problem I might have to face. Except for one.

"Hey," I whispered. "I gotta ask you a question, and I don't want you to lie to me, okay?"

"Of course," Debbie cooed. "Talk to me. What's on your mind?"

"Listen . . . some of the guys—like Richie, Pete, and Perry and them—think that Gino might be a . . . you know . . . a *fairy*. What do you think about that? You've met the kid. How do you see it, Deb?"

"Why?" she said. "Because he wasn't very good at *kick-ball*?"

"You watched through the window while we played?"

"I watch you every time you play," she said.

"Oh man," I said. "Now, I'm gonna be embarrassed every time I play ball across the street."

She twisted her beautiful body so that she was looking right at me, while the raft was floating uneasily. "I didn't forget about our deal next June second," she said. "On our birthdays. And I hope you haven't forgotten either. We're doing this, A.J."

I could barely contain myself in my denim cutoffs. "I can't talk about it. You're gonna make me wanna push up the date."

We laughed as loud as two kids who had a secret from the world.

"Seriously," I said. "Before he comes outside, what do you think?"

"Do *you* care?"

I didn't have to think about that too long. "I couldn't give a shit less," I said. "It's a little aggravating dealing with the guys in the neighborhood, but as long as he's happy . . . I'm happy. I mean, what does it all mean anyway?"

"Then screw it," Deb said, before planting an open-mouthed kiss flat on my mouth that tasted like candy. "You can handle it."

"Whoa, whoa, whoa," I said. "What was that all about?"

"I don't know," she said, real coy like, while sliding out of the raft and climbing up the steps. And then she finally let her veil down. "Don't look at *me*. I'm just as nervous as you are." She laughed.

"Hey," I said. "Seriously, *how* can we wait until *next* summer?"

"I don't know. Lemme think about it," she said, as she climbed the fence. "But you got your hands full right now. And, by the way, the Coogans are still hanging out at the curb. They're so creepy." She blew me a kiss with her right hand pressed to her lips. I just let myself sink to the bottom of the pool, and I sat there for a while until my ears hurt from the water pressure and I ran out of breath. When I pushed myself up for air, I saw the unmistakable image of my father, home early from work, with a look on his face that would want to make people change their zip codes.

"Dry off, lover boy. We got a situation," he said. While Debbie and I were rolling around on the raft, he'd already come home and changed into cutoff jean shorts and his favorite terry-cloth V-neck shirt. As I hopped out of the pool to dry off, I could tell by the speed and seriousness of things happening in the house—my mother's anguished face and Gino already standing in the foyer ready to go—this seemed like some sort of perilous mission we were needed on.

My parents and I met Gino in the foyer, with my mother wringing her hands and my father breathing hard through his nose.

"What is it, Dad?" I asked, concerned. "Is anyone in trouble?"

"All I can tell you is we aren't the ones in trouble," he said. "I come home early to enjoy the pool and I gotta see this shit on my sidewalk."

"What sidewalk? What happened?" I said.

"Come with me; walk out to the front yard. And when you tell me who did this to our house and to our family, I'm gonna fuckin' mop the floor with them."

Gino and I followed my father to the front white sidewalk outside our lawn, and there they were in blue chalk, the ugly words: GO HOME QUER. The culprits missed a letter, but my father was gonna make sure they didn't miss the lesson. And with his .45 caliber handgun very visibly stuck inside the back of his shorts, he was hell-bent on finding whoever was responsible for pulling this off, in broad daylight no less.

"Al," my mother pleaded. "A *gun*?"

"Lilly, go inside." And she turned back into the house.

He knelt down to me on the lawn, "These pricks need to learn a lesson, you understand?" Gino was shaking like a leaf. "I think I have to throw up," he said. "I really think I have to throw up."

"Then throw up," my father said. "Now . . . do you have any idea who might have done this? Before I break somebody's head, I gotta know—without a doubt—who we're dealing with here."

"Well," I started, "the Coogan boys were outside the house while I was in the pool. And they can be pricks sometimes, Dad. And they *were* sitting outside our house earlier. It's gotta be them. Yeah. The Coogan boys."

"Show me their house," he said, with absolutely no anxiety and, actually, a quiet resolve.

And with that, Gino and I held each one of my father's hands and walked six or seven houses down the street, all the while with my father's .45 in his back waistband and impossible not to see with our peripheral vision. Gino and I looked at each other, and it was a bonding moment. This was something we were all in together. As a family. Gino looked like hell, and I could've used a few Tums, if you want to know the truth.

Our next-door neighbor was Joe D'Ascoli—Pete's dad—and he was a New York City cop. Maybe he spotted the gun or something, but in the middle of watering his lawn, he piped up, "Anything wrong, Al?"

"Nah. Nothing to worry about," my father said.

Mr. D'Ascoli went back to watering his lawn, and we continued down the street.

A few seconds later, my father stopped us and asked me a very simple but scary question.

With a sinister yet comforting smile creasing his face he said, "Which house? Point."

We walked down the street for maybe a minute while my father whistled—*he whistled*—until I stopped walking and pointed at the brand-new colonial-style home that the Coogan family had just moved in to.

"This is it?" he said. "With the goddamn statue of the niggah lawn jockey holding a lantern? What an asshole."

"Yeah, Dad," I said, startled, embarrassed, and excited at the same time. "This is Danny Coogan's house."

"Uncle Al," Gino pled. "This is not a big deal. You don't have to get mad at this family."

My father lovingly rubbed Gino's cheek with his hands. "Gino, do you understand what those pricks wrote on the sidewalk? Listen to Uncle Al. We have to nip this in the bud. Those words are ignorant and wrong. And it's not gonna happen at my house."

"But it doesn't matter," Gino said. "Those boys don't know me."

My father shrugged his shoulders, and it looked like he was admiring the beautiful weather around us. He was completely calm when he said, "Well then, let's get to know each other."

I was shaking when we walked up Danny Coogan's driveway and finally reached his front door.

"What the hell are you shaking for?" my father asked me. "Did *you* do anything wrong?"

"No."

"Then stop shaking," he said.

Like most of us in the neighborhood, the Coogans had a screen door separating them from the outside world. No one locked their doors in my neighborhood in 1974, so seeing a flimsy screen door was nothing unusual. My father knocked a few times, and I tensed up. Gino was turning gray and was close to shitting his pants.

Mr. Coogan answered the door. "Can I help you?" he said, with a slight smile on his face.

"Hiya," my father began. "We haven't met. My name is Al Benza. I live a few houses down on Snedecor."

"Yes, yes," Mr. Coogan said. "Nice to meet you. Why the visit?"

"Well," my father said. "It goes like this: there are some terrible words written with chalk on the sidewalk in front of my house, and my son says your boys are the ones who did it."

Mr. Coogan gave off a quizzical look. "How's that?"

"You heard me," my father said. "Why don't you get your sons to come to the door and ask them what they did."

"I have a *great* idea," Mr. Coogan said. "Why don't you go back home and think about what you're doing here, blaming my boys for something they didn't do."

"Are you calling my son a liar?" my father said.

"I'm saying it would be a *great* idea if you just walked away, and I'll forget this ever happened."

Within a second, my father dropped Gino's and my hands and punched Mr. Coogan with his right fist in the face, straight through the screen door. And a second later, he was inside their home, standing over a stunned Mr. Coogan, with a gun to his head.

"You gotta a lot of '*great* ideas,'" my father huffed. "But the best thing you're gonna do now is call your sons downstairs or else I'll pull this trigger and we'll see all your 'great ideas' on the wall behind you."

Gino wasn't in Hackensack anymore.

With that, Mr. Coogan—who was understandably out of breath and low on courage—called for his sons to come to the foyer and see him lying there in such a prone position. "*Danny, Marty, Tudor . . . come downstairs now,*" he said. It sounded like he was moaning and shrieking at the same time.

When the boys arrived, they had no idea what they were walking into.

"Dad," they screamed. "Are you okay?"

"Never mind that," Mr. Coogan piped up. "Did you write something on the Benzas' sidewalk? And *don't* lie to me!"

Once the boys sheepishly admitted what they had done, my father let Mr. Coogan up, uncocked his pistol, and stuck it back in his waistband. "Okay," my father said. "See how easy that was? Now, just have the boys come by and wash that shit off my sidewalk and we'll have no more problems from here on in."

The Coogan boys stood there frozen.

"You heard the man," Mr. Coogan shouted to his sons. "Go clean up your mess, for God's sake. And then I'll deal with you idiots later!"

"I'm sorry it came to this," my father told him. "I'm not the type to hold a grudge. So this'll all be water under the bridge now that your boys are doing what's right."

"Yeah, yeah," Mr. Coogan replied, straightening his shirt and plastering his hair back on his sweaty head. "Of course, of course."

As we walked back home, Mr. D'Ascoli—who'd obviously seen the entire confrontation—stopped watering his lawn. "Everything all right, Al?"

"Yeah, Joe. The guy just fell down in his hallway."

"I could've sworn I saw him swing at you first, if I'm not mistaken," Joe said.

"Could be. It all happened so fast," my father said. "I got some clams for you in the icebox."

"Beautiful," Joe said. "Some cherrystones would be great."

"Yep. No problem."

Before we even got home, the three Coogan boys were already scrubbing the ugly words off the sidewalk with a big brush and a big bucket of car wash. And as the sentence disappeared, my father was already offering the boys some barbecue and a dip in the pool.

"When you boys are done, why don't you take a dip?"

"Yeah, no . . . it's okay, Mr. Benza. We gotta go," Danny said.

"Well, take a frankfurter with you for chrissakes. They're good, like Nedick's," my father said, imitating the famous Giants and Knicks broadcaster Marty Glickman.

Needless to say, the Coogan boys didn't have much of an appetite. My father had Gino and me stay out on the lawn until the ugly words disappeared and washed away into the street and down into the sewer. When the sidewalk was just about clean and the phrase was gone, the Coogan boys walked away knowing they could never, ever mess with us again. But I'll tell you this: Danny Coogan and I remained friends for years and our families never had a problem again. No cops were called on that ugly day. It was pure and simple street justice. Gino and I watched them turn the corner.

"That's that," I said. "You know my father did that for you, right?"

"I think I know," Gino said, looking down at the sidewalk.

"Gino, I want you to know something," my father began, while uncoiling the garden hose. "Sometimes a person can hurt you without putting their hands on you. And sometimes that hurts even worse than a black eye. You understand what I'm saying?"

"You mean like name-calling and stuff," Gino said.

"Name-calling is bad enough," he said. "But it's even worse when the names they call you aren't even true."

"Yeah, like queer," I said.

"But those kids are your friends," Gino said.

"Not anymore," I said.

When I said that, Gino's spirits seemed to lift. He looked toward my father, who was hosing off the last remnants of what had been written on the sidewalk. "Real friends don't do things like that," my father said. "And I'm here to make sure they never do anything like that again."

"Yeah," I told him. "Blood is thicker than water."

"And it sure as hell doesn't wash away as easy as chalk."

"So," I said. "You still feel like throwing up?"

Gino thought about it for a second. "Actually, no. I feel . . . better."

That was the moment I think we turned a bigger corner than the Coogan boys did.

10

SUNDOWN

The July Fourth weekend was upon us. We always had a full house, especially on that holiday, since my father's birthday fell on the fifth. So it was always like a double party—with friends and relatives coming from all parts of Long Island, Jersey, and the five boroughs. My mother, sisters, and Frankie cranked out food like crazy. Forget about chicken wings and six-foot heroes. We made deep trays of lasagna *and* manicotti *and* linguini with fresh pesto sauce. Our kitchen was as busy as a crime scene, with Frankie preparing veal marsala and some shrimp francese. Rosalie was prepping a huge fisherman's platter, with clams that I, and after some practice Gino, had plucked from the bay with our own hands and feet. At the same time, I had my father frying the cardoon—a rhubarb-type stalk—that he would find growing wild on the off-ramps of the highway. My mother would cook for an hour or so at a time before she gave in and stood knee-deep on the third step of the pool to cool off. Then she would head right back into the kitchen. Some of my crazy relatives, like Anthony Coniglione and Phil Mattera, brought in trunkloads of fireworks that we shot off all day long, while escaping the occasional drive-by from Suffolk County cops. We always had a ton of stuff to blow off. We had mats of Black Cat firecrackers that we shot off in a big aluminum garbage can. We had M-80s, Ash Cans, whistling rockets we inexplicably called "niggah chasers," and tons of bottle rockets that we shot out of a steel pipe hammered into the lawn. And, maybe funniest of all, we had Roman candles that we would light and aim at each other's asses. I remember Gino laughed like crazy as we aimed our rockets at his ass while he tried to successfully get out of the way. We usually spent the whole day using flimsy punks to light the explosives, but for the big show at nighttime—the one that brought out the relatives and neighbors—we used lengths of slow-burning rope that lasted all night. For years on end, we were always able to finish the night with a beautiful firework called a Silver Jet that would mysteriously knock out the streetlight in front of our house, rendering our part of the block completely black.

My father would applaud the show the wildest, whistling with both pinkies in his mouth. And then he would beckon several people up to our second-floor outdoor sundeck for the night's dangerous finale. Most people would peel away, but there were always half a dozen of us or so who would climb the stairs and watch him ceremoniously stand on our sundeck, outside the master bedroom, as he fired off live ammunition up to a mile away into the purple night of the Great South Bay. First he'd use his .22 rifle, and then he'd finish off with the carbine with the cool World War II scope. Didn't it occur to him that someone might be sitting on their boat some-where out there, enjoying a beer, and suddenly get picked off by a stray bullet? Didn't it matter what my mother said or my relatives urged? No. It was ceremony, and it reminded him of the five years he'd served in the European theater. There was no stopping him. So people just sort of held their breath for the twenty-one shots to end.

Gino and I plugged our ears for the first several shots or so. He spoke up as my father was changing rifles. There was the slightest bit of his being a wiseass when he started uncontrollably laughing and said, "He's probably killed some people tonight. If tomorrow's newspaper has a story of a per-son dying on their boat by a bullet to the head, Uncle Al is the murderer!"

As the night wore down and the fireworks faded in the black sky, there were always a couple of stragglers who'd show up at our house just to be a part of *any* part of it. My father had a wonderful habit of collecting people, and Sun-days and holidays were the days they usually wandered in. I can remember all sorts of characters dropping by, like my father's buddy, Danny DiSalvo, a down-on-his luck lounge singer, who always had a $5 bill for me whenever he popped in, smelling of whiskey and trouble.

A few years earlier, my father had taken my mother, my sister Lorraine, and me to see Danny sing old standards at a dive bar in the Bronx called the Wagon Wheel. There was decidedly nothing *Western* about it, except for the fact that the Bronx was considered the "Wild West" in the seventies, on account of its high crime rate. I remember the place basically being a two-story gin mill—with nothing going on (far as I could tell) on the second floor. The tables were all shaped and fastened like wagon wheels, but the entire joint had indoor/outdoor, wall-to-wall *carpeting*, and even at my young age, I could tell that didn't look right, feel good, or smell nice. The fact that my father took me there—on a school night, no less—was something else. And to make matters worse—Danny didn't start singing until some guy "in charge" of lighting found him with a giant, five-foot spotlight the second he walked out of the kitchen door singing the first bars of "The Boulevard of Broken Dreams," with all the sad swagger of a washed-up Tony Bennett.

"Watch, A.J., watch," my father told me. "Listen to the words. Listen to what the lyricist wrote. It all begins with a writer. No words, no song."

And I listened. And that night stayed stuck in my head. A man I barely knew, belting out the first bars of the song by a foggy window beside the swinging door of the kitchen next to a bar.

I walk along the street of sorrow!
The boulevard of broken dreams.
Where Gigolo and Gigolette
can take a kiss without regret,
and so forget their broken dreams.

I was hung up on two things. Where was the "boulevard of broken dreams" and who were Gigolo and Gigolette? But I kept it to myself for a bit. Then, after what seemed like a ten-song set, Danny kissed and hugged us good-bye and we got in the car and headed home. It had to be close to midnight, because my mother kept telling me, "Close your eyes, A.J. Go to sleep. You got school."

But I had to speak up.

"Dad," I said. "Remember that song about Gigolo and Gigolette?"

"Of course," he said, lighting up, peering at me in the rearview. "That's a classic."

"Is the boulevard of broken dreams real?"

"You bet your ass."

"Where is it?"

My father told me, "Look out the back window. You see those tall buildings?"

"Yeah," I said, seeing parts of the Manhattan skyline through the cracked plastic back window of his convertible.

"That's the place," he said.

Danny wasn't the only lost soul we let in after dark.

There was also a very sexy, raven-haired, sad sack of a woman named Maureen, who our door was always open to after we had witnessed a married man throw her out of his slow-moving car right in front of our house one night. "Don't you understand?" he hollered. "It's over, you bitch! You come by my *home*? Where I live with my *wife* and *kids*? I'll make sure you disappear!" Before my father could get the guy's license plate, Maureen ran up our driveway, crying her eyes out and screaming suicide. I remember her mascara running down her face and under her chin. We took her in. Gino was astonished while my mother poured her coffee, lent her an ear and comfort, and insisted she sleep in our guest room for that night until she had a clearer head in the morning. She was screwing a married man, and he was trying to break it off. Even I could figure that out. But, at one point, when she was sobbing and looking like she'd been through hell and back, Gino went to the bathroom and came back with a hairbrush.

"I'm going to brush her hair for her," he told me softly.

"Yeah?"

He walked over to Maureen as she was relaying her story of love, lies, and deceit and held up the brush to her.

"Can I . . . do you want me to . . . should I brush your hair for you?"

"Oh my *Gawd*." Maureen sobbed in her Long Island accent. "How sweet of you. Good luck, doll. I'm a fuckin' mess."

"This is my nephew Gino," my mother said.

"Oh, he's so goddamned *precious*. Please stay this sweet," she said. "Don't become a prick like all the rest." She had a way of stretching syllables.

Gino looked mesmerized as he brushed her crazy hair straight while she laid out her story for all of us around the table that night.

And then there was my father's "connected" friend "Big" Freddy Muserella—who had worked as a bone breaker for the Anastasia brothers' crime syndicate. He loved coming by, all three hundred pounds of him, because my father was the only guy he let bust his balls. Freddy would stammer through a horrifying story of street justice, and my father would get a kick out of interrupting him.

"And *when* . . . Storio Longo," my father said over espresso and anisette. "You tell me stories about snuffing out gangsters for the Anastasias, but you're scared shitless of a little duck in Rosalie's backyard. What kind of a hit man are you?"

This ruffled Freddy's feathers.

"That's no ordinary duck! The thing flies three inches off the ground and comes right at me, nipping at my shoes," Freddy said. "I'm gonna put a contract on that fuckin' duck."

On nights when Freddy felt like confessing, he'd tell Gino and me about how bad guys had to be "handled." He'd pull us in real close and explain his signature move—one which Gino listened to, though it definitely made him queasy. "So . . . for the guys who couldn't keep their traps shut," Freddy said, "I'd lay the guy on the street, with his *mout* open and his front teeth biting the curb. And then, you know, I'd just step on his head. Boom. No more teeth."

"That's so badass," I said.

"Oh my God," Gino said. "That poor man."

"Well," Freddy would reason, "you can't do too much talking with no more teeth in your head."

But one of my father's friends who was a bit calmer was a younger man named Nolan. At first, I didn't exactly know what he did for a living, but I remember my father initially having a hard time telling me what Nolan's occupation was.

"Dad, what does Nolan do for money?"

"Sales."

"What kind of sales?"

"He sells stuff that falls off the truck," he'd say.

"What stuff is that?"

"You know . . . *hot* stuff."

"I still don't get it, Dad."

"All right . . . then no more questions, A.J."

It didn't take too many visits to figure it out, especially when he dropped by on my father's birthday very late at night with a dozen or so five-gallon cans of Gino's Italian Ices sitting in his backseat, covered with a bedsheet. He had them in every flavor, even in blue—whatever flavor that was—and all the kids at the party came running to the driveway.

"Only the best for the Benzas," Nolan shouted up the driveway to my approving father. "Gino's!"

"Now I've seen everything, you crazy bastard—*hot* cold ices." My father laughed.

"Who, me?" Nolan said. "Nah, I got a guy who knows a guy. . . ."

We were all happy to see Nolan, though there was always some sort of calm to him. Whatever it was, it made the women, as well as the men, love to laugh with him. His stories were a bit on the softer side, and he knew to always stay even with my father in terms of his place at the table, but never to pull ahead.

Nolan was always good to me, but that summer he was especially sweet and understanding to Gino.

"I can't stay long," he said to my father. "But I'll see you Thursday night. Let's get in the boat and catch some crabs. The gas is on me."

Nolan was like that. He came and went.

"He seems nice," Gino told me as he left.

"Yeah . . . he's cool."

"Do you think he'll really come back Thursday?" Gino asked.

"Yeah, if he says so."

Sure enough, on Thursday night—about two hours before we could even catch crabs at nightfall, Nolan showed up to get ready for our excursion.

"You're early," my father said. "Have some wine while we get the boat ready."

I was standing with Gino at the edge of the shallow end of the pool, trying to teach him to not be afraid of diving into the pool. Gino stood there shaking in his shorts, while I stood behind him and held on to the waistband of his shorts and begged him to lean over and dive.

"Just put your toes on the edge, Gino. It's four feet; you know you can't drown," I said. "What the hell are you so scared of?"

Gino stood there on the edge and gently pushed his toes to the end of the coping. "I can't do it. I just can't," he said. "Let's try tomorrow. I swear I'll do it tomorrow."

"You've been saying that for a month," I yelled.

Nolan laughed to himself as he walked over and stood on the other side of the pool.

"Gino!"

"Hey, Nolan." Gino smiled.

"Gino, listen," Nolan started. "Bend your knees a little, and bend at the waist a little . . ."

"I know how to teach him," I said. "I been diving since I was six." Then I whispered in Gino's ear. "You can do this for yourself. I'm holding on to your shorts, I won't let go. Just put your toes on the edge, bend your knees a little, squeeze your ears with your arms, okay?"

He got in better position and began to lean a few more pounds of himself over the edge of the pool this time. "Don't let go," he hollered.

"I got ya; I got ya," I said, "Come on, bend over, squeeze

your ears, and point your head toward the water. You got this!"

Just as his shaking almost overtook his whole body, Gino did everything I had asked. The checklist was complete. All he had to do was fall forward and wait for me to let go of his shorts. "I'm ready . . ." he screamed. "Here I go!"

He leaned his whole body forward and was in perfect position to beautifully slide into a dive. I let go at the perfect second, only to watch Gino's arms pull away from his ears, point his chin to the sky and smack his body hard on the surface of the water. Splat!

He came up from under the water a second later. "Did I do it? I think I did it," he screamed.

"Does your belly hurt?" I said.

"Yes, it's killing me. Does it always hurt when you dive?"

"No, Gino," I said. "It only hurts when you *don't* dive and you do a belly flop!"

"Oh . . . I'm sorry. I thought I had it."

"That's okay," I said. "We'll get it right."

While he was watching us and drinking from a jelly glass, Nolan opened up a shopping bag filled with brand-new Topps baseball cards. The ones that came with the dusty wafer of bubble gum in the pack.

"Look at this," he said to Gino and me, as he dumped the goods on the backyard patio. "Baseball cards. You gotta look though. There might be a Lou Piniella in there!"

"Oh, this is so cool!" I said, as I ripped through the bounty.

Gino went searching but didn't quite know what he was looking for. Nolan picked up on that and began to help him. "Let's see what you got in this pack," Nolan said. "Nah. Nah. Nah. Yeah . . . Bobby Murcer. You hold on to that card. He'll be a Hall of Famer."

"Who's Bobby Murcer?" Gino said.

"Don't worry," I interrupted, while shuffling through my deck of cards, with a mouth full of bubble gum. "I'll tell him."

By the time we pushed the boat off the dock and headed down the crooked canals toward the bay, Nolan and Gino had bonded to the degree that Gino was actively listening to Nolan telling him how to scoop up crabs. My father was at the wheel, while Jack and Frankie manned the most important spots—on the bow, with the long nets and their giant handheld flashlights plugged into a car battery on the floor of the boat. I stuck to the back of the boat, my mission being to catch any crabs that escaped Jack and Frankie's angle. Gino and Nolan worked the other side of the boat, but I could tell my father wasn't expecting too much out of them. In the middle of the boat there stood a garbage can. It worked this way: crabs like to swim near the surface at nightfall. If you were good with the flashlights, you could spot some fifteen yards away and direct my father as he was slowly meandering in and out of the bridge's concrete pillars, which was no easy task.

"Pop! Pop!" Jack would say. "Ten feet to the right . . . ten yards ahead, I got my eyes on three right on top of the water."

"Okay, okay," my father would say, through a cigarette in his lips. "Here we go. . . ."

And that's the way in went all night. Whatever Jack couldn't reach, Frankie scooped. And vice versa. Maybe every ten minutes or so, I'd hear the guys tell me about a crab they missed. "A.J. . . . coming your way," they'd yell. "Port side, two feet deep, a big muthafucka. Don't screw it up!"

And I'd get ready, with my smaller flashlight and longer crab net, as my father backed up the boat in tiny spaces while forty or fifty other boats were doing the same thing. It was maddening at times. I'd barely catch any at the stern because a crab would usually dart down to the bottom of the bay within a second if you reached and whiffed on it.

"Damn it," Jack would say. "He was right there."

"Sorry."

"All right," my father would assure me. "Let's get the next one."

Meanwhile, on the starboard side of the boat, Nolan was teaching Gino how to hold a flashlight and a net. And it was Nolan—amid our maddening desire to fill the trash can with blue claws—who helped Gino scoop up a couple of crabs that might've gotten away. It was Nolan who taught Gino, on the spot, how to tell a male crab from a female crab. And it was Nolan who explained the oddity of catching a soft-shell crab. It was all stuff Gino would've learned back at the house, but Nolan's soft-natured coaching slid Gino into a different groove. To what extent, it wasn't yet apparent.

11

SPILL THE WINE

There came points during summer vacation where I didn't want to spend every single second outside, where every game or far-flung idea was a way of measuring our skill at sports or neighborhood mischief. It wasn't as if I was tired of the competition or scared of the challenges that my friends and I would put before one another. It was, plain and simple, a much better way to let Gino have me to himself. And in so doing, I felt like I could make his vacation much more memorable and less harrowing. Whenever I thought back to that teary phone call Uncle Larry placed to my house or the excursion to the sporting goods store or any one of the times my father shot me that look that said, *Take care of your cousin*, it just seemed like the thing to do. It was only right. If I expected Gino to be front and center for all the crazy things my family, my friends, and I did or said and, more, figured him to just soldier on as if he were one of the guys, then I was going to have to do some of the activities he'd been asking me to take part in for weeks on end.

"Hey, what time does that show on PBS *Hodgepodge Lodge* come on," I asked him out of the blue.

"What? Why?" he said, barely containing himself.

"You want me to watch it, right? It's your favorite show."

"And . . . you're saying you want to watch it. With me?"

"Well, I ain't watching it all alone," I said.

He was acting like a caged puppy when they see you walking toward them with food.

"Okay," he said. "Let me put on channel thirteen right now and see. It's always on. I'm sure it's on. What if it's not on? Are you saying you only want to watch it with me right now, or whenever it's on . . . ?"

"Calm down, calm down, calm down," I said, laughing. "Just switch the dial to thirteen."

And sure enough it was on. And before me was the sight of a woman, the host of the show, which always made me flip the dial really quickly whenever I was making a pass and checking to see if the more-mature program *Zoom* was airing.

"There's *Miss Jean*," Gino shrieked. "It's on. It's on."

"All right now," I said. "What am I watching? What happens on this show?"

Those simple questions, or more precisely, my interest

in *his* interests was to Gino what an intense game of stickball was to me.

Gino went on to breathlessly explain that Miss Jean would let everyone in on the wonders of nature. As we sat there and watched one episode and then another and then, to his insane delight, one *more* episode, I got the gist of what she was doing. This Miss Jean—as dowdy and masculine as a lesbian in Timberlands—would spend thirty minutes opening up a pinecone and exploring its depths in the hopes of seeing a beetle or worm. Or she would examine the habitat of a hedgehog or a red fox. She was always gentle in her approach to nature and, looking back, might have even been one of the leaders of our modern conservationist movement. But, boy, was she boring as fuck!

"Isn't she interesting?" Gino said. "I think she's beautiful."

"You think that's a beautiful woman?"

"Well, if not beautiful, then *very* pretty."

"All right, okay," I said. "We been sitting here in this room—which is as hot as my balls—for ninety minutes. Can I show you who I think is beautiful?"

"You mean Debbie next door, right?"

"How do you know what I feel about Debbie?" I said.

Gino smiled a bit. "When we play flashlight tag, you and her disappear for, like, a half hour," he said. "And I just figured you were sitting someplace real dark and talking and stuff."

"And stuff?"

"Well"—he squirmed—"you know . . ."

"Yeah, sure, I get it," I said. "Look, I think Debbie is hot, but she's young, ya know? I'm talking about showing you a beautiful *woman*. I wanna see if what I show you does the same thing to you as it does to me. I wanna see what happens."

"Well, what's gonna happen?" Gino said.

"Just wait."

We went upstairs and I laid chest down on the rug and fished out a *Playboy* from way back beneath my bed. I don't even know why I hid the things. My father always had *Playboys* strategically placed around the house—in his master bathroom, next to his living room recliner, in the trunk of his car, et cetera. He made no bones about me opening one up. In fact, I think he wanted me to.

But there I was on the floor, moving aside an old pair of roller skates, an erector set, and a chemistry kit until I laid my hands on the box containing the board game Candy Land.

That was where I kept my stash.

"What is that?" Gino said nervously. "Is that a naked-lady magazine?"

"Yep. The best kind. *Playboy*. And it's a good one."

I put it on the floor and started flipping the pages.

"It's hot in here," Gino tried. "You wanna go in the pool for a while?"

"Soon," I said. "I want you to see this girl—"

"What about Aunt Lilly?"

"She's cooking. Besides, we can hear her coming a mile

away. It takes her ten minutes to climb those thirteen steps. Relax."

I flipped the pages slowly, passing a couple of pictorials before I kept it cracked open to the centerfold, which featured Miss July 1973, Martha Smith. (A few years later, Smith was in *Animal House* and appeared in a scene with her shirt getting ripped off to reveal her white bra. I remember she had her hair up and wore long, white, cotton gloves. That's what first got me hooked on her. Not my type at all—a little on the short side, blond, and a real WASP. But who has control over their first movie crush?)

"What do you think?" I said.

I watched Gino take it all in. He was actually amused, not shy at all, which surprised me.

"Let me flip through this for a second," he said, giggling.

"Have a ball," I told him, as I put the mag on his lap and I shuffled through the box for another issue. I carefully watched as Gino turned from the very first page all the way to the end, where they kept the naughty comic strip *Little Annie Fanny*. Then I watched him go through it from back to front, as he stopped on some things and breezed past others. It was in those little moments, when we each had a *Playboy* in our hands, that I cheated to see where Gino's eyes stopped. I saw he stayed on pages longer that featured handsome men selling Pierre Cardin cologne or Barbasol shave cream or YSL sports coats. We were reading the same magazine, whose very purpose touted a "lifestyle for men." In those moments, it was now obvious that Gino and I might be headed for two very different lifestyles. At least in our heads and lustful hearts, anyhow.

"A.J., Gino . . ." my mother shouted up the steps. "Peter and some other friends are at the door. Come on down."

"I'll put these right back in the same spot if you ever wanna look again," I said. "You don't have to ask me, just reach way in the back, inside the Candy Land box."

"Umm, okay," Gino said. "What does Pete want to do? Do I have to play if it's kickball?"

"Believe me," I said. "After last time, kickball is the *last* thing we want to play."

Most of the bad things we did that summer were hatched next door in Pete's spit-shined two-car garage. Whenever Pete's father was walking the beat on an overnight shift in the city, his mother was usually busying herself with housework or long chitchat sessions on the kitchen phone. Sometimes she'd be upstairs with her eldest daughter, Joanna, watching *Kojak* or whatever popular TV show was on that night. The last place she'd visit was the garage. Maybe she was afraid of what she'd see. For whatever reason, she never ventured in. Never knocked on the door, nothing. But it was the kid who was suddenly tagging along with Pete that made this night a bit more dangerous. I didn't want to scare Gino, but the "new" kid among us was Vinny D'Avanzo. Vinny was a kid who had moved into the neighborhood a year ago, and he was still convinced he had to do some stupid, daring things in order to be accepted in our clique. He had a cute eleven-year-old sister named Tina who was always like a shadow to him. On this particular night, Vinny was dying to hang out with us but he couldn't shake his sister. So, in his own twisted, little mind, he devised a plan that we could all hang out in Pete's garage and be okay with Tina's company.

On many occasions, Pete's garage was like an after-hours club. There were nights we all sneaked in bottles of any type of liquor we could smuggle out of our houses. One night we even passed around a bottle of old, spoiled vermouth. Another time, we watched Richie Tischler blow smoke rings with his brother's unfiltered Camels. When we felt really crazy, we'd creep to the hallway on the second floor of his house and jump down the laundry chute and land in the heavy-duty hamper in the corner of the garage. It was a straight drop. I don't know how we didn't break our backs.

But that night was different. Gino and I followed Pete and Vinny to the garage and were quickly met by Richie and Perry, who were flipping baseball cards on the driveway. Vinny took us all aside before we entered the garage and gave us the skinny. Only God knows how he got this out of his mouth.

"Hey guys, hold up, hold up," Vinny said, with a slight smirk on his face. "Tina wouldn't disappear. I can't shake her tonight. And my mom says I gotta watch her . . ."

Tischler was the first to pipe up. "Then what the hell are we gonna do with that little cockroach snooping on us all night?"

Vinny took an approach that put a stink on diplomacy, let alone family values.

"Listen, *listen*," he said. "I told her she could hang out for a little while, but I asked her what price she was willing to pay."

"And what'd she say?" I asked.

And here's where nothing makes sense at all, but—years later—it would become one of those handful of nights a boy never forgets. However she figured it out—maybe with a shove from Gloria Steinem—but Tina knew she, as a young girl around a bunch of boys, was holding a better hand. She laid out her deal points to big brother, and he explained them to our confused, frightened, and timid souls.

"So . . . Tina wants to hang with us guys tonight," he said. "And we all know my little sis is cool, right?"

"Yeah, right, yeah," we all mumbled.

"Well, here's the deal," he said. "She said if we let her hang out with us for a night, she'd take her shorts off and show us . . . her *beaver*."

And there it was. One minute you're sitting in your hot bedroom flipping through *Playboy*, trying to figure out life. The next, your cute, little neighbor—who you've known since kindergarten—is offering up her private parts as a way to fit in with the boys. Between Debbie's promise and Tina's offering, I was happy, excited, and sick to my stomach all at the same time. Gino was as white as the sheets in the hamper.

One of us, I can't remember who, started laughing wildly.

"What the fuck are you talking about? Where? When? She's just gonna pull her shorts down in the garage?"

"No," Pete said. "Here's the deal: she's behind the azalea and rhododendron bushes right now. She won't do it in the garage with all the lights on."

She had her scruples.

So, once we composed ourselves the best we could, we all marched quietly to Pete's backyard and lined up right by the giant bushes, where Tina was lying on a blanket, out of our view, with her shorts off. Fortunately, for us, the moon was glowing strong enough that we didn't need the bright lights of the garage.

Pete parted the bushes and we ducked in one by one. None of us had seen one in the flesh before. Tischler went first, Perry second, I was third, and Gino last. It was like a receiving line. Tischler was already in and out and laughing really loudly as Perry dipped behind the hedges for his ten-second view. By the time I walked in and knelt next to Tina, I could feel the other boys' faces staring at me through holes in the bushes. I didn't like the predicament I was in, since I really liked Tina. She was a brown-skinned, pretty girl—almost as dark as I was—because I think she was Sicilian on her mother's and father's sides. When it was my turn to do whatever it was we were supposed to do, I sat down beside her and touched her tight, flat belly and I looked in her eyes and tried to figure out her motive. It was nothing like the *Playboy*s up in my room. Tina's area was so small and delicate and, with her little bikini lines glowing in the dark, I could barely make out any hair at all, but I took a good, long look. As beautiful and vulnerable as she was, I did what all the boys did: I just stared at what she was nervously presenting to us. She looked me in the eyes and giggled uneasily, then covered her area with her hands as if to say, *That's it, show's over.*

On the other side of the hedges, I had to adopt the macho stance. There were high fives all around, and I remember me and the other boys trying to suppress laughter from our brimming smiles. But that wasn't really how I felt. I really wanted to wrap a blanket around her and put a stop to it, but my stupid standing among the boys made that choice harder than what you'd expect.

"Let's go, Gino," Richie shouted. "You're up!"

By the time Gino walked into the hidden area, smelling of pine needles and fresh earth, we were all poking our faces in to see what he'd do. I watched him kneel down, touch Tina's face, pluck a nearby dandelion, and awkwardly place it on her privates while whispering, "I'm so sorry." Tina's expression changed on a dime as she hiked up her panties in record speed, got up, and headed out of the yard and down the block. I also saw Gino bolt for the front door of my house.

"That wasn't supposed to happen," Perry said. "That's it. Show's over?"

"Yeah, man. Let her go," I said, with a little bit of anger. "What the hell else you want her to do? Huh?"

The guys just backed up and acted as if it were time to

move on to the next thing. Obviously, for Gino and me, it was something more important.

"What's up with Gino?" Perry said.

"I don't know," I said. "Maybe it freaked him out. I keep telling you guys that he's only ten."

I left the boys behind and caught up with Gino at my house. I took the steps upstairs two at a time, where I found him in our bedroom, pacing back and forth.

"You all right?" I asked.

"That poor girl," he said. "I can't believe that's the way he treats his little sister."

"It ain't like that. He loves his sis," I stammered. "But, did you at least like it? Was it something you'd like to do again?"

"No," Gino said adamantly. "I don't understand the big attraction. It's just not something I enjoy seeing—in a magazine or in person." We continued the debate as best a twelve-year-old and a ten-year-old could, but it went nowhere, and before long Gino crashed on his cot.

I tried reasoning a bit. "Gino, I don't know what it's like in New Jersey or with any of the boys you hang around with," I said. "But, I'm telling you, that was something that a guy dreams of. I mean, I feel bad for Tina and all, but she volunteered. And we got to see her bush in person, right up close. I'd never seen one, had you?"

"Maybe some boys are like that, but I'm not one of them," he said. "I don't know how I'm going to be able to look at her tomorrow."

"It'll be a little weird," I said.

He turned his body toward the wall and asked if I could shut the light on the way out. "I'm really tired. Let's just forget it for tonight."

"Yeah, yeah, sure," I said. "It's been a long day. I'll come up a little later."

When I got downstairs, I could hear the unmistakable snippets of my mother gossiping with Aunt Mae and Aunt Mary around the kitchen table. With a large Entenmann's crumb cake before them and their second pot of coffee brewing, chances were good they'd be occupied for a while. Rather than walk into that sit-down, I decided to follow the sounds of the living room TV, where my father was all settled in his recliner, with our wonderful mutts, Sonny and Pippen, asleep on his lap.

"Hey, Dad," I said.

"There he is," he said. "The man with the plan. What's the plan tonight?"

"I don't know," I offered.

"Well, I do," he said. "You've got two free hands and your father needs 'magic fingers.'"

"Yeah, sure, Dad," I said. "The lotion is right here."

"Good."

"But . . . Dad," I stammered. "Is it okay if I ask you some advice about what happened tonight with Gino and some friends of mine?"

With that, my father sat up, pushed the dogs away, and let me know his mind was 100 percent there for me.

"But of course," he said. "Tell me what's what."

To his credit, my father never made it difficult to discuss things of this nature. And so I began, while spreading all sorts of lotions on his tired body and giving him the right type of rubdown.

"So, it goes like this," I started. "Tonight, Vinny D'Avanzo allowed Tina to show us her beaver behind some bushes in their backyard. It felt weird and all, but I just did it because all the other guys were doing it."

"Was it more embarrassing for you than for her?" he said.

"I'm not sure," I said. "She didn't seem too upset, but it really seemed to screw up Gino's head."

"How so?"

"Well, the minute he saw it, he put a flower on it and told her how sorry he felt for her. And then he just ran back home and crashed in his cot."

"Have you talked to him?"

"Yeah," I said. "I tried, but it seems like he wants to block the whole thing out of his mind."

"Let me ask you a question," he said. "Do you think, after spending some time with Gino, that he's the same kind of boy as you and your friends?"

"No. He's not," I said. "He's a great kid, but he's different."

"Yes," my father calmly said. "And I'm pretty sure he's going to stay that way because he doesn't have a choice."

"That's okay, as long as it's okay for him," I said.

"Well, A.J., it might not always be okay for him," he said. "But if he's brave enough to get through this himself, then I want him to always feel it's okay for him to be who he is whenever he's around this family. Do you understand?"

"Yeah, sure, Dad," I said, somewhat confused but satisfied with my father's on-the-spot verdict.

"Hey, Dad," I said. "Mommy said aunt Geneva is feeling better from her operation and might be driving to our house in a few days. Maybe that will make Gino feel better."

This is where my father had had enough of the charade. "I'm sure it will. But A.J., listen to me, your aunt Geneva didn't have cancer like your mother had two years ago," he said.

And staying true to his form of never hiding the bitter truth with a sugar coating, my father decided it was time to cut me in on it.

"She had a *voluntary* hysterectomy."

"But why?" I said, remembering all the pain my mother endured during her illness. "Why would someone go through the pain Mommy suffered if they didn't have to?"

He held his tumbler of Scotch, resting it on his belly, before letting me in on a dark family secret. "She didn't want to have any more of my brother's children."

I stood there in the silence, stunned by the violent honesty of what he said. I reached for more lotion and continued his rubdown.

12

<hr>

MIDNIGHT AT THE OASIS

God only knows we had our share of neighborhood arguments and physical altercations during the summer, and as much as my father wanted to show us his calmer side, there were some situations that had to be handled in his inimitable style.

Enter George Coulter, an unfortunate man, though a man of considerable wealth, who lived on the canal and just happened to be hosting a catered affair in his backyard complete with a waitstaff in black suits and white gloves. The party was occurring one Sunday afternoon, a beautiful August day, about twelve houses down the canal from where we lived.

If I could get into my father's head, I'd imagine he was holding the piece of information from us that had really set him off in the first place. Apparently, as the story goes, Mr. Coulter was unhappy with his recent home-carpet installation, but rather than speak to my father man-to-man, he had the nerve to drop a note of his disapproval in our mailbox and refer to my father as a "hotheaded guinea" in the process. Mind you, my father was merely the manager of the carpet store. He had nothing to do with installation.

I'll never know how long my father let this bit of information fester in his brain, but I don't recall anything different when it came to prepping the boat for a fishing expedition. Everything was the same. While the men got the boat stocked with the correct fishing poles, nets, and baits and also made sure we had a half dozen or so clamming bags on board, the women prepared tin-foiled sandwiches to bring to the boat, as well as water, soda, and various bags of chips and stuff. And, of course, several flasks of Scotch were lowered into the boat.

When we pushed off the dock, I couldn't help but see a glint in my father's eyes.

After he instructed Jack to man the anchor minutes after we had set off down the canal, we knew something was up.

"You want me to grab the anchor, Pop?" Jack said. "What's going on?"

"Don't worry, just listen to your father-in-law," he said. "We're gonna drop anchor right around the corner. Teach this fucker a lesson in front of his family."

"What's going on?" Gino asked me.

"Just don't worry about it," I said. "The old man knows what he's doing."

Soon as we drove about one hundred yards and were smack-dab in front of Coulter's fancy backyard party, my father instructed Jack to drop anchor in the canal.

We sat there for a few moments, watching the Coulters' fancy party, from twenty yards away or so. "The Girl from Ipanema" was playing on his fancy, backyard hi-fi system.

"Is this going to be a fight like at the Coogans'?" Gino asked me.

"You never know," I said.

After a few minutes of watching champagne served with finger sandwiches, my father had seen enough.

He cupped his mouth with his hands and shouted at the host and his guests.

"Attention, ladies and gentlemen. Attention all. George Coulter is a *cocksucker*! The man whose house you're at is a scared cocksucker who'd rather stick notes in people's mailboxes than talk to them in person."

With our boat drifting toward the dock, my father was attempting to climb atop the guy's property. That's when Coulter appeared at the dock and did all he could to appease my father and beg him to meet him the next afternoon.

"Al, please, there are women and children here. . . ."

"Attention, women and children . . ." my father started.

"Please, God, stop," Coulter said.

"I'll stop," my father said. "Do your friends know about your fuckin' letter-writing skills?"

"Al . . . please. I was wrong. Let's please settle this tomorrow."

"Say you were fuckin' wrong again"

"Al . . . *please!*"

"Say, 'I'm a cocksucker and I was wrong!'"

"I was wrong. Jesus Christ, I was wrong."

"Say it or I'll hop up on your fuckin' deck right now."

"I'm a . . . cocksucker, Al, okay?"

My father put one foot on his dock.

"Okay, okay. I'm a cocksucker . . . and I'm wrong."

"Good boy, George," my father said. "Come see me at noon or else I'll show up at your house with a fuckin' baseball bat. Understood?"

Needless to say, Mr. Coulter complied, quickly saw things our way, and apologized profusely.

After we lifted anchor and had traveled a few minutes down the canal, Jack laughed. "Hey, just another lazy Sunday afternoon."

"The thing that gets me," my dad said. "There was no stamp on the letter. That means the prick had the balls to stand on my porch and drop it in the mailbox."

"No respect," I said.

By this point in the summer, Gino had grown accustomed to my family's untimely outbursts of anger, love, passion, and insanity. I can't say he ever felt comfortable joining in, but just seeing his stoic face while my father tangled with Coulter was worth a million bucks. Watching him being able to maintain his emotions made him feel more like a brother to me.

As we meandered down the canal, Jack and Frankie were talking about heading out to the Sore Thumb, an area that featured the bigger fish because of its vicinity to the biggest inlet to the ocean. As they talked and imagined the type of doormat fluke they might hook in to, they were setting up their fishing poles.

"Whattya say we stay local and grab some fish and clams and head back home early and make the women happy?" my father said.

Jack and Frankie wanted no part of that. "Pop," Frankie said. "I just hooked up three poles with a squid and killie combo and a four-ounce weight. Let's at least give it a shot in the deep water."

"Yeah," Jack said. "I feel it, Pop. Look at this high-low rig I just put together. There's no way we head back home without hooking in to some fluke and bluefish."

My father laughed. "You and your Puerto Rican rigs. If you weren't so good to my daughter, I'd throw that whole pole overboard."

Their enthusiasm got the best of my father and as we exited the canal, he opened it up the engine, with the bow of the boat lifting like a rocket as we headed out to the deep, dark fertile waters of the Sore Thumb. We rode the waves that day and followed all the charter boats way out where the Atlantic

Ocean flows into the Great South Bay, and mostly suffered the gigantic tugs that the big, invisible fish put on your line. That type of action is usually enough to stay out there, but there comes a point, when the bait runs low and your patience is sapped, that you have to turn your boat toward home.

Jack and Frankie had caught just enough fish and seen enough action that they were satisfied with our excursion, and listening to my father's idea of heading back was an idea they were now open to. They were standing in the stern of the boat, filleting the thick fluke and beautiful bluefish we caught, on the boat's cutting board, while lofting the bloody remains into the air for the screaming army of seagulls that were floating above us.

"Guys, don't get rid of the sea robin," my father said, referring to a prevalent and ugly bottom-feeding fish that had wings and whiskers and actually grunted—almost *argued* with you—once you brought it aboard the boat.

"Pop," Jack said. "I'm not gonna let you eat that fish. Come on, we have enough fluke and blues for a week."

My father would have none of it. "Let me tell you something. I don't believe in discarding a firm-fleshed fish. You take a grilled or pan-fried piece of sea robin and you throw it on some Italian bread with a slice of tomato from the garden with some lemon mayonnaise—and you got a meal fit for a king."

"It's still early, Pop," Frankie said, tossing the entrails of a small sea robin fish into the air. "And we still have some bait left. It'd be a shame to waste it."

"Keep the bait out of the sun," my father said. "We can use it in a little while. First, I want to make a stop somewhere."

"Where we going, Dad?" I said. "Gino and I are feeling a little seasick with these waves."

"Just keep your eyes on the bridge, something stationary, and you'll be fine," he said. "I'm gonna take you somewhere where the water is flat like a mirror."

My father took us through the Dickenson Channel, a challenging bit of the bay that had a sea floor that could rise to a depth of fifteen feet from twelve inches within seconds. You had to really know what you were doing and trust your crew like hell or else risk chopping your propeller to bits by taking big bites out of the bay's floor. We were headed to a small dot of forgotten land some hundred yards away when my father masterfully cut the engine and relied on Jack and Frankie to use long poles to guide us toward what looked like a scaled-down version of Gilligan's island. We were no more than fifteen minutes from home, but we might as well have been somewhere in the South Pacific.

When we finally got close enough and were floating in less than two feet of water, my father hopped out of the boat and asked Gino and me to join him and pull the boat by the anchor until we were on the lip of what looked like some sort of magic fishing hole.

"Dad," I said. "What is this place? Why haven't we ever come here?"

"I was waiting for the right time," he said. "If the tide is too high, you'll never see it. If the tide is low enough—like right now—you never forget it."

With each step in the crystal clear water, Gino and I were elbowing each other as we got closer. We didn't care where we stepped or what creature might lie in wait. Gino and I felt like we were walking toward heaven. And for the first time that summer, Gino had actually stopped walking a couple of times to bend down and pluck clams from the bottom.

"Atta boy, Gino," Jack hollered.

"We gotta hurry," Gino said. "I think I see a wooden diving board in the middle of that island." He'd come a long way from being afraid to slide down my father's leg into three feet of water. Now Gino was actually walking ahead of me by a foot or so.

I cupped my hand above my eyes. "It *is* a diving board. What is this place?"

And with that, we took off. Running as best we could in knee-deep water, parting the occasional patch of seaweed, and trying to be the first to—what felt like—colonize this mysterious marsh that seemed to exist solely for us.

"This place looks like a woman's perfume ad," Gino gushed. He was onto something. It didn't smell like a woman ought to, but with warm, Caribbean-type water and a big, thick diving board that some good soul had anonymously built for other families to enjoy, it certainly was twenty years ahead of Calvin Klein's TV ads for Eternity. But this wasn't an infinity pool in some rich guy's backyard. This was nothing more than a glorified fishing hole tucked within a tiny island of land off the beaten path of red and green buoys in the middle of the Great South Bay. While my father, Jack, and Frankie were raking in clams with their hands and feet, Gino and I finally hit land some thirty yards away. The water we dived into—off the big, thick, plank—was colder and much deeper, but it was clear enough to spot baby eels swimming by, as well as the inevitable blue-claw crab feeding on the bottom. And just when things couldn't get any more extraordinary, we saw a family of seahorses—which were many miles away from where they were usually found but obviously just as enchanted with the spot as we were.

I felt like I was gonna see Jacques Cousteau and the *Calypso* turn up any second.

"Gino," my father shouted. "Get some mussels; find some starfish. Bring me back something we can take home and show the girls!"

That was the summer before *Jaws*, so absolutely no one was afraid to dive into a mysterious, deep-water hole and go exploring. We got so brazen and so drunk on fun, Gino and I decided to surprise the men and jump off the board bare-assed naked. We got a couple of horns from passing boaters, but we couldn't care less. This was the most fun we had all summer. And when Gino finally got the nerve to pry a starfish off the side of a rock, he held it above his head for everyone to see. "Uncle Al," he hollered. "Look! Look!"

"Beautiful," my father shouted. *"Atta boy!"*

Gino stepped onto the marshland, stuck the starfish to his chest, and screamed out, "I'm Sheriff Benza, goddammit. And this is my land!" He was so happy. I don't think he even remembered he still had his shorts off.

It was a beautiful moment, wrapped within a wonderful day. Gino was more than at peace with himself at that spot. It was as if the water made everyone equal.

It was almost impossible to tear us away from that spot. But with the tide coming in, our little oasis was vanishing inch by inch. We didn't want to believe it, but we could see it with our very own eyes. My father whistled for us to come back aboard.

"Ah, crap," Gino muttered.

"Ah, shit, is right," I said, pulling my shorts back on.

We followed the anchor line back to the boat, stopping to grab a couple of clams on the way in. When we were on board, my father lit up a cigarette and told us we had one more stop to make before we headed home. "Nothing can top that spot, Uncle Al," Gino said, kissing my father's cheek. My father smiled gently, pulled Gino in closer to him, and told him to take the wheel.

"Just go nice and straight," he said. "I'm right behind you. I'll tell you where and when to turn."

"Can I curse?" Gino asked us out loud, over the hum of the outboard.

"Of course," came our reply.

"*Holy shit!* I'm driving a boat." He laughed.

My father took the wheel back in the deeper water. He was a good uncle; he wasn't crazy. As we headed east and nearer shore, my father was aiming the boat toward a tiny canal that had signs posted all around: PRIVATE PROPERTY and KEEP OUT. The sun was setting so that the sky on the horizon looked like a mix of orange and pink sherbet. This was always when the anxiety in me kicked in. *Where the hell are we? Is someone going to confront my father? Do we have enough gas? Is my mother worried about us?* But a couple of stolen glances at my father's eyes always settled me. He seemed to be more at ease in dangerous situations. But, still, I am also my *mother's* son.

"Dad," I said. "Should we be here? Can we get arrested?"

Jack and Frankie laughed. "Yeah," Frankie said. "This can get us heavy time. Driving down a private canal? How many years can that get us, Pop?"

"Ten . . . maybe twenty years," my father said. "Depends how many fish you pull out of here."

"Yeah, right," I said, turning to an equally anxious Gino.

"If *you're* scared, then how should I feel?" Gino piped up.

"I'm all right," I lied. "At least we aren't gonna see any clowns."

"Or dolls with busted eyes and wooden teeth." Gino laughed.

"Lines in the water, men," my father told Jack and Frankie nice and quietly. "We might even get a few weakfish in here. I see them breaking water."

My father cut off the engine as we drifted down this beautifully cryptic canal with stately waterfront homes to our left and right. All we could hear were the last of the stubborn seagulls sitting on poles and the sound of the men casting out and reeling in their shiny lures.

"Where are we," Gino asked.

"This is Sayville," my father said with a bit of reverence. "And all the people in these houses don't want us here."

"So why are we here?" Gino said, as he swatted away a swarm of mosquitoes dancing on his hair and face.

"I want you to meet someone," he said. "If she's home and she sees us, believe me, she'll leave a mark."

As we neared the end of the canal, and Jack and Frankie had managed to wrestle in a couple of beautifully colored weakfish, the boat came to a mysterious stop in front of what looked like the back of the White House if it were built on the water. And then, as if on cue, we heard a small engine starting up and within a few seconds an elderly woman was tear-assing toward us in her golf cart right to the edge of her property to make a stand.

"Here she is," my father said, his eyes lighting up.

"Here *who* is?" I said.

"Julia Thorne."

As it turns out, Julia Thorne was an eccentric eighty-year-old widow who was somewhat of an infamous recluse. My father knew about her only because he had stumbled down the canal years earlier and had gotten a verbal whipping from her for trespassing. But, ever the romantic, the next weekend he drove down her canal again. But this time he brought her steamed clams and mussels to make up for it. They went on to forge somewhat of a crazy relationship. He would play the hapless boater, and she would play up the irate homeowner. But it had become a familiar game to the both of them, unbeknownst to me. This trip was purely to introduce her to Gino and me.

Mrs. Thorne got out of her golf cart, wearing a giant floppy hat and a thin scarf around her neck. Her hair was long and thick and red as heartbreak, and her eyes were pale blue, almost silver. As she walked toward us, the huge gold bangles she wore bounced from her wrist to her elbow. She held a bullhorn but never bothered to bring it to her mouth. She didn't make too many appearances outside her home, but when she did, she made sure her performances were memorable.

"What are you mutts doing on my property?" she demanded. "Every fish you catch, that is, if you even have the mental capacity to know *how* to fish, belongs to me. Me, Julia Thorne, 315 Mayhew Street, Sayville USA."

"This is crazy," Gino said. "Are we at Greta Garbo's house?"

"Do you understand me?" she demanded. "Are you all slow or retarded?"

As far back as my childhood went, this was obviously another one of the people my father collected. From the sad to the spiritual to the far-flung, he knew them all.

My father had a hard time stifling a laugh. "Signora Thorne," he said, "my nephew Gino here didn't believe a beautiful woman like you existed. My brother drove him all the way from New Jersey to see you and your magic fishing hole."

She put down the bullhorn and snapped open a butterfly fan and fanned her face a few times, taking a glance in Gino's direction.

"That boy is too precious to have your wild Sicilian blood pulsing through his veins, Al." She called Gino to the dock and onto her property to have a better look. "You're lucky you look like Leonard Whiting in *Romeo and Juliet*," she told him. "Now tell your uncultured uncle that unless he gets me fluke fillet, I'll have his dago ass arrested for trespassing. And the policemen here are all my friends. I call them and they come."

"You don't want to do that," he told her, smiling.

"Why, it is. It is. It is what I want to do."

At this point, with Jack and Frankie even chuckling, I knew we were dealing with a fun, crazy old broad. She was harmless and she loved the company, and my father knew that about her. But she did have Gino hostage on her property.

"What's it gonna be, Al? The fluke or this fella?"

My father gave Frankie a wink and a nod before climbing on her dock and handing her a bucket of fluke meat and a couple dozen clams. Thorne inspected the bounty before giving my father a tender smack on the chest. "This'll do." She laughed. "Come back anytime, but not anytime soon."

"I love you too, signora. Ciao, *bella*!"

"Oh, bullshit, you do!" she yelled over her shoulder. "You think you're the first sailor to lie to me?" Then she climbed in her cart and sped off like a maniac.

My father and Gino hopped back in the boat, we flipped on the lights to the bow and stern as we made our way back up the canal and turned the boat west toward home.

Later that night, Gino ate my father's Sicilian pizza, steamed clams, and fluke fillet with as much enthusiasm as the rest of us. By the time we were done, we couldn't get to bed quick enough. We were spent. A whole day on the bay will do that.

"Julia Thorne looks like an old movie star," he said. "I *love* her."

"She's a classic, I gotta say."

Before he dozed off, Gino whispered, "I feel like Julia Thorne is my favorite actress, and she's not even an actress! Does that make any sense?"

"A lot of things didn't make sense today," I said. "You had a starfish on your chest with your pud hanging out."

When I turned to share a laugh with him, Gino was already out. A slight smile creasing my little cousin's sleeping face.

ROCK THE BOAT

My father made it his point to leave work and get home a little on the early side as the summer went on. He was always happiest entertaining people, and with Gino staying with us, it sort of made my father feel like he had a captive audience to perform to. And I don't think anybody loved it more than I did. I had spent so many nights of my childhood trying to keep my eyes open as my father split his sales job at 10:00 p.m. and finally arrived home around a quarter past. But it was the ritual leading up to his arrival that helped keep me awake. First, my mom or I would open the garage door around nine thirty, so he could pull his Mustang inside and walk in the house through the side door. And once he stepped from his car, he usually started to jingle the coins he had in his pocket, so even if I had dozed off, that unmistakable sound of loose change would snap me awake. Not to mention our dogs would start to go wild at the sound the keys made in his hand. And then, once he finally stepped inside the house, the energy he gave off—whether it was through a joke, a compliment, or a complaint—gave me another hour or so of life.

"A.J., you're lucky," Gino said with a hint of envy. "At least you get to actually see your father every night and hear him tell you all these great stories. Try being the son of a very busy doctor."

In the summer of 1974, it wasn't just me who waited anxiously for my father to come home. It was becoming more and more apparent that Gino was also doing all he could to be there for his entrance and what high jinks might lay ahead. And that didn't go unnoticed by my father. So there were many nights when he might have passed up a sales commission or two, just so he could spend some quality time with us boys.

He came home really early one night, took a few shots at the basketball hoop with us, and then ran into the house to change clothes.

"Dad, what are you doing home so early?" I said, passing him the ball.

"I got things for us to do," he said.

Even my mother was shocked at how early he was home. "Was it that slow at the store?"

"Can't I *do* something with my son and my nephew?"

"*Yes!*" I said. "What are we doing?"

"The Bay Shore Theatre is showing a double feature of *The Cowboys* and *The Omega Man*. John Wayne and Chuck Heston. It doesn't get better than that. Go get cleaned up. Nolan's gonna meet us there and hold our seats."

My father disappeared upstairs to change while Gino and I washed up in the bathroom. "I know *The Cowboys* is a Western," Gino said, "but what's the other one about?"

"It's like a science fiction thing," I said. "Whatever. It'll be good. Wait till you see this theater. It's huge and it has a giant chandelier in it."

"Oh . . . I love chandeliers," Gino said.

"I figured you would."

"Um . . . can I sit next to Nolan?" Gino asked a bit shyly.

"Yeah, whatever, I don't care."

"It's just because I'll probably have questions and he's so nice and likes to help me with things."

"Yeah, yeah. We'll work it out."

The Bay Shore Theatre was only a few miles away, across an ugly stretch of road where Montauk Highway gave way to Main Street, which over the years had given way to a porno theater, a junk shop, a great Jewish deli, and a couple of naughty bookstores. There was some sort of mental-health facility nearby, because at various times of the day, these miserable people would walk the streets in various states of breakdown. If you weren't used to it, it could make you feel somewhat uneasy.

"Uncle Al," Gino said. "Is it safe around here? We just passed a man with his pants down, spinning in circles on the sidewalk."

"Oh, yeah, that's 'the Swinger,' " my father calmly replied. "I see him every day. He's harmless, but I've never seen him with his ass out."

A few blocks later we came across "the Screamer," an old, white-haired man who liked to lean into the street and yell at slow-moving vehicles. I remember "the Screamer" never being at a loss for words but not ever caring if the words he strung together were making any sense to anyone besides himself. "What happens to people like him?" I asked my father as we passed by his sidewalk pulpit.

"I can't say. Sometimes . . . people just snap," he told us. "Life gets too hard; they lose people they love . . ."

"You'd think their family would take care of them," Gino said.

"Not everyone has a family. That's why family is so important," my father said, looking in the rearview mirror. "Family can make you feel wonderful or it can be a real pain in the ass." As he said that, he whipped his right hand off the wheel and began tickling Gino and me at every vulnerable spot on our thighs, knees, and stomachs. "*You love your family?*" he shouted.

"*Yes, yes!*" we shouted back. "*Please . . . stop!*"

"I can't hear you guys. . . ."

"Yes," we screamed. "*We love our family!*"

That was my father's way of getting our minds off the crazy people wandering around our car. When we finally parked, paid for the tickets, and had our Cokes and popcorn, my father took us by our arms into the darkened movie theater. The previews had already begun. We could barely see a few feet in front of us after coming in from the bright streets. And, never caring about making a scene—too large or too small—my father yelled out for Nolan.

"Nolan!" he said quickly and loud enough to hear over the flickering projector.

"Down here, Al," came a reply a few rows back. "Follow my whistle."

And we did. And, thankfully, nobody got upset. We settled in. Gino sat next to Nolan, and I squeezed in between him and my dad, who was sitting on the aisle.

It was a long, exhausting experience. *The Omega Man* opened the evening, and *The Cowboys* closed it out. I remember the whole theater letting out hoots and hollers the first time John Wayne's face filled up the screen. I wasn't much for Westerns, but my father had always used John Wayne as the right measure of a real man. His character in this movie was a lot like the roles Wayne had played before. Only this time, he wasn't in Iwo Jima or at war anywhere. He was a rancher named Wil Andersen, who lost his ranch hands to the gold rush. And being forced into finding replacement riders for his yearly four-hundred-mile cattle drive, Wayne begrudgingly hired local schoolboys. He taught them how to rope, brand, and herd cattle and horses. There were plenty of fights and scuffles along the way, but I was getting the message loud and clear—that my father wanted me and, mainly Gino, to see how boys grow into men or confirm their manhood through acts of violence and vengeance. *That* part of the movie, I loved. It was the movie advertisement that made me feel like Wayne was going soft. The actual advertisement for the film just didn't play right in my ears: "All they wanted was their chance to be men, and he gave it to them. The youngest was nine. There wasn't one of them over fifteen. At first, he couldn't stand the sight of them. At last, he couldn't take his eyes away."

I noticed Gino was leaning forward in his seat enthralled, while I was somewhat disappointed. This wasn't starting out as a typical John Wayne flick.

"Dad, what's this all about?" I whispered. "The Duke with little boys?"

"Just watch, just watch," he assured me.

By the end of the film, my father was nudging my elbow and softly squeezing my arm when the boys were tending to a dying Wayne, the victim of a knife fight. Wayne tells the boys how proud he is of them. "Every man wants his children to be better than he was," Wayne says as he fades away.

There were some sniffles in the theater, but none louder than Gino's. Nolan comforted him a bit outside on the way to the car, and again sitting at our dining room table once we got home and were discussing the films. As usual, Nolan was especially sweet and understanding to Gino. And Gino, a few nights earlier—and quite bravely—confessed to me that he felt a special bond with Nolan. There was absolutely no hanky-panky going on—and Gino was never alone with the guy—but, from what I could see, he was just a man who listened intently to Gino's feelings and responded in a kind and gentle manner. But to Gino, Nolan's visits meant more. That night changed everything in my father's eyes.

"It's okay you cried, Gino," Nolan said. "I got a little choked up too. Did you notice?"

"No . . . but I really wasn't crying. My eyes were watering a little," Gino said.

Nolan laughed some, pulled Gino closer to him, and mussed his hair. It came off as an awkward attempt to comfort him.

That moment seemed a bit out of place for me. Nolan wasn't blood and, for my liking, wasn't close enough to the family to show that kind of affection.

I watched my father's posture change somewhat for the worse when Nolan pulled Gino in. I saw the muscles in his jaw clench a bit while his eyes seemed to go flat. I changed the subject as quickly as I could, saying how much better I liked *The Omega Man*.

"Come on," I said. "*The Omega Man* ruled. Heston had to deal with a plague from China, a cult of albino mutants who are out to kill him, and the whole time he's going crazy. That's a lot more exciting than a bunch of kids helping John Wayne with his cows."

"But *The Cowboys* is saying so much more," Nolan tried to explain.

"And Heston got to kiss a black girl," I said, sensing I could redirect the anger bubbling within my father that was about to be channeled toward Nolan.

"Easy does it," my father said, firing his first salvo over my bow.

"Gino, my boy," Nolan said. "You'll understand what John Wayne felt when you're a little older. He loved being around those boys for a lot of reasons. Trust me."

"Well . . . maybe A.J. is right," Gino said, pulling away from Nolan a little. "There was a lot going on in *The Omega Man*. I think I was just getting tired at the end of the night."

Nolan lowered his head to be eyeball-to-eyeball with Gino. "Look at me," he said, squeezing his nose between his fingers. "*The Omega Man* was garbage. John Wayne made men outta all those dumb kids. He was the best thing that ever happened to them. Without him, they'd be nothing."

My father slowly pushed his chair away from the head of the table and stood up. "Well, it's getting to be that time," he said.

"Ahh, already?" Nolan said, checking his diver's watch.

"Yep."

"No ices tonight?" Nolan tried. "A.J.? Gino? Tell Uncle Al he's a stinker." He let out a loud laugh, expecting us to join in. But he was met with silence from our side of the table.

"Nah," my father said tersely. "I gotta measure a house at seven a.m., and the kids gotta hit the rack."

"Ahh . . . then that five-gallon can of lemon ice is gonna go to waste, Al."

This wasn't a typical good-bye in my house. There was too much distance between four people in such a tight space. And too much silence between the words.

"It's not gonna go to waste," my father said.

"Sure it is, Al," Nolan said as he stood up.

"No it's not, Nolan," my father repeated. "Because you're gonna take it somewhere else."

Gino and I stared at the ground as my father walked to the kitchen freezer. I could hear him wrestling the can out of the back of the box. Then he walked to the front door, cracked open the screen, and cocked his head for Nolan to follow. Nolan didn't even look at us as he slowly peeled away from the table and began to meet my father in the foyer. "Al . . . what's going on? Was I out of line? I don't understand. . . ."

"No more ices, Nolan," he said. "When I need some, I'll find you."

When my father shut the door that night on Nolan, he immediately turned the dead bolt. For a man whose front door was always open to anyone, this message was clear as a bell.

In my twelve years as Al Benza's son, I could have taught a master class in what I had learned from my father's nuances and gestures and fragile Sicilian code. And what I picked up was Nolan most likely overstepping his boundaries when it came to his role—not only around my father, but more important, around Gino and me. His attempts to be almost paternal to Gino just greased the wheels for his quick exile. You didn't have to know my father for more than a few minutes before you understood he didn't need any assistance protecting his family. And most of all, he had no use for any other man assuming anything close to resembling a parental role when it came to his son. Or, in this case, his brother's son.

"And that's that," he said, shrugging his shoulders as he turned from the front door and joined Gino and me at the table. "I didn't like seeing a man trying to change your mind, Gino. Trying to make you feel something you didn't want to feel. That's why I did what I did. And that goes for the both of you. Don't ever straddle a line. It's a dangerous place to be."

"Uncle Al," Gino began to sniffle. "But I lied. I *did* like *The Cowboys* better. Nolan was right. And now I feel bad he's gone because of me."

My father picked up Gino and sat him on the table.

"Okay, okay. Don't cry," he said, kissing his head and wiping his cheeks. "It's okay. There's no right or wrong answer. I just want you to have your own reason, not someone else's reason. Do you understand? Uncle Al is not mad at you, Gino. I just want you to stand up for yourself and be comfortable in your own skin. Life's gonna hurt you if you're not."

Gino could only get a few words out at a time in short

bursts because of his emotions. "I . . . liked both . . . movies . . ."

"Okay," my father said, holding him.

"But it's just easier for me to understand what the young
boys felt for John Wayne than it is for me to think of the end
of the world. The boys loved John Wayne in the movie. I *loved*
John Wayne in the movie. Didn't you, Uncle Al?"

"Yes, yes, yes. Anyone who doesn't love the Duke in a
movie can go to hell," my father said, cupping Gino's cheeks.
"And I love that you love him too. And what's most important
is you had the balls to say that yourself. Nobody made you say
or do something you didn't want to. You were yourself. Do
you see the difference?"

"Uh-huh." Gino sobbed. "But Nolan is your friend. And
now he's gone because of me."

"No. Don't worry about Nolan. There are a million
Nolans. He knows why he's gone."

"But why *is* he gone?" Gino said.

My father hugged Gino to his chest and looked at me
over my cousin's shoulder.

"Nobody needs to make up your mind for you," he said.
"You understand?"

"Okay," Gino said, a bit muddled inside my father's arms.
"All right."

"You know who you are?"

Gino's red eyes darted toward me and then locked straight
onto my father's. "Yes, I do," he said.

"Okay," my father said. "Are you gonna tell me who you are, or should I ask somebody else?"

"No." Gino began to smile.

"Well . . . who are you?"

"I'm Gino Benza," he said, laughing his throat clear.

"Oh, hello, Gino Benza. And what kind of movies do you enjoy?"

"I like *The Cowboys*," he said.

"Really? Why would you like that crap?"

"Because . . ."

"Yeah, yeah," my father said, straightening him out by the shoulders. "Because why?"

Gino looked over at me for some type of go-ahead or approval.

"Tell him," I said. "Tell him exactly what you think."

"I liked *The Cowboys* because the boys made John Wayne . . . nicer," he said, searching for the right adjective. "The boys made him a better man. And he died happy."

"That works for me," my father said. "Now, gimme a hug. And tell my son Chuck Heston kissed the colored girl only because she was the last woman on earth."

14

BAND ON THE RUN

When my mother recovered from her hysterectomy, a year earlier, it took her two weeks before she was up and at 'em and back to work at her household chores without so much as even a grimace. But for some reason, Gino's mom, Aunt Geneva, needed two months to do the same. That's why it took her so long to finally muster up the strength to decide to hop in her car and make the drive from Jersey to check in on her boy. When she placed a call to my mother and told her she was finally feeling well enough to come by for a surprise visit, my mom welcomed her with open arms and was thrilled she was feeling up to it.

My mother, who was absolutely terrible at keeping secrets, couldn't help herself and rounded up the family to make the announcement of Aunt Geneva's upcoming arrival.

"Okay, okay, everyone listen," she said, as she hung up the phone. "That was Aunt Geneva on the line. She says she's feeling better and she's coming on Sunday to see all of us. She misses Gino very much and wants to come for the day. Isn't that great, Gino?"

Gino looked a bit dazed at the news. "She was just on the phone?"

"Yes. And she can't wait to see you."

"Did . . . she want to talk to me?" he said.

"No. She wants to surprise you," my mother said. "But I'm telling you ahead of time."

"Mom . . . why are you telling us the surprise?" I said. "You just ruined it for Gino."

Whenever my mother was flustered, she immediately acted indignant. "Well, what the hell do you want me to do? I don't know what time she's coming. I don't know what to cook. I gotta make sure this house is clean. We gotta be prepared."

"Okay," I said. "Now we all know Aunt Geneva is coming. Are we supposed to act surprised?"

"Of course," she said. "She told me don't tell anyone!"

Gino and I laughed together. "All right, Ma. We don't know nothin'. Great plan. So when is she supposedly *not coming*?"

"Sometime Sunday morning," she said.

"Great," I said. "I'll make sure we act *shocked* when she drives up."

"Thank you. *Jesus Christ*, is that so hard?"

On the day Aunt Geneva was set to show up, Gino and I were on the driveway, shooting baskets as we got ready for her big "secret" arrival.

"How am I supposed to act?" he asked me while rebounding my free throws. "I haven't seen her for weeks. Should I scream and jump up and down? Should I cry or something?"

"Definitely don't cry," I said. "She'll think you're having a rotten time out here."

"Yeah, that's true," he said. "But how do I act *fake* surprised?"

I stopped shooting hoops and sat down on the basketball on the driveway and gave it some thought. "Okay, let's see," I started. "What kind of car does she drive?"

"A blue one."

"No, but what kind? Is it a Cadillac? A Buick? A station wagon with wood panels on the sides?"

"I just know that it's blue," he said.

"Oh, Christ. So whenever we see a blue car headed down the street, we'll just act all regular like we have no idea what's going on. And if it slows down at the curb, and we see your mom hop out, then we gotta act surprised as hell."

"I can do that," he said.

"Yeah, but the problem is there are gonna be a *million* blue cars passing the house, cuz."

He promised me he'd recognize it when it got near.

"So, let's see how you're gonna act surprised," I said.

"Um . . . I guess I could jump up and down and be like, *'Oh my God, Mom. What are you doing here?'*"

"Eh . . ."

"And, you know, *'Oh my God . . . I missed you so much.'* All that stuff."

"Yeah, okay." I exhaled. "You *do* miss her, right? I mean, just a few weeks ago you were locked in the bathroom, on the toilet bowl, crying to her."

Gino thought about what I said for a few seconds. For the first time in a long time, I didn't see his eyes welling up whenever the topic turned to his family.

"It's just weird to me," he said above the neighborhood noise of ice-cream trucks, lawn mowers, and boys working under the hoods of cars. "I guess I'm homesick, but I wish I could figure out why my sisters and father couldn't take care of me at home while my mom got better."

"Well, you told me how busy your dad is and all," I said, trying to smooth things out. "And, well, you know how much my family loves having people over."

"Yeah . . . I guess."

"Just don't think about it so much," I said. "In an hour or so, a blue car with your mom will drive up and you'll see how much she loves you."

"*God* . . . these allergies," Gino said, wiping his wet eyes.

"They're not allergies," I said, punching his shoulder. "You cry when you're sad. So what? Big deal."

"No . . ."

"Yes, ass!"

Gino laughed a little. "I'll be fine. I'm fine."

It wasn't ringing true to me, so I called in some reinforcements. I had the Rossitto girls come over from next door and make the driveway look a lot more crowded and fun. I figured a bunch of pretty girls would put Gino more at ease and make the eventual mother-and-child reunion go smoothly. Plus, I was always up for having Debbie around me.

"Here's the thing," I said to the Rossitto girls—Debbie, Yvonne, Eileen, Julie, and Diane. "Gino's mom is coming from Jersey to make a surprise visit. But my mother ruined the surprise, so now we have to act shocked when she drives up."

"Okay . . ." Debbie said. "What do you want us to do?"

"I don't know. I'm thinking we can all play basketball together so Aunt Geneva sees Gino has been having a good time and all."

"Why hasn't your mom come by sooner, Gino?" Julie said. She was nine.

"She had an operation and she had to get better first," Gino replied, taking the ball away from me, dribbling to the basket, and shooting a layup with decent form.

"What kind of operation?" Julie asked. "My mom's a nurse, so I know a lot about diseases and cancer and stuff."

Gino gave me a look, begging me to take over.

"She had, uh, you know, *lady* surgery," I said. "Same as my mom did last year."

"Was it cancer?" Yvonne asked.

Gino stayed tuned out, throwing up shots at the hoop.

"I don't know. Probably. Maybe," I said.

Then the youngest Rossitto, Diane, piped up. "Is she gonna die?"

When Gino heard that question, he didn't even bother catching his rebound. He stomped back to the fray. "No," he said. "She's already home and getting better. She's not going to die."

"She ain't gonna croak," I told the girls, loud enough for Gino to hear. "My mother made it. So will Aunt Geneva. It's no big whoop."

"I know," Julie said slowly. "But I always hear my mom talking about cancer. And that's pretty serious."

I gave Debbie a look that begged of a boy needing help, and she quickly rounded up her sisters and calmed them down.

"All right, enough of this crap," I said. "Nobody's dying. Matter of fact, she's driving right now and will be here any minute. Can we all just play basketball and have fun? What else do you have to do?"

It was as desperate a plea as I had ever made. But I had to, seeing how every turn in the conversation, every mention of surgery or death, was wreaking havoc with Gino's fragile emotions. This was supposed to be a happy time. Deep in the folds of my heart, where my father's words played like a calliope, I knew I had to keep him stable and strong.

We had been playing hoops for a few minutes and, sure enough, a slow-moving blue Impala pulled up to our curb. And Aunt Geneva stepped out wearing a loose-fitting, floral print muumuu.

"Ma!" I yelled through the screen door. "Aunt Geneva's here."

It turned out all the plans Gino and I had discussed went to waste because the moment Aunt Geneva walked up the driveway, Gino ran to her and hugged her hard around her waist.

Her first words were: "Oh, honey, don't squeeze Mommy too tight. Gently, gently."

I stayed back by the basket and watched.

"How are you?" she said to him. "Let me look at you. I swear you look taller! And we'll see about getting you a haircut."

"Hi, Aunt Geneva," I hollered.

"Hello, hello, A.J.," she said. "Look at you. So tan. So lean. My God, you really are your father's son."

"I missed you, Mom," Gino said, trailing her up the lawn.

"Well, I miss you too. And who are all these pretty young ladies?"

The ever-polite Rossitto clan ran up and introduced themselves.

"Well, I have to say, you are all such beautiful girls. Are any of you Gino's age?"

Julie put up her hand. "I'll be ten in nineteen days."

"Wow. That's wonderful. Gino, did you know that?"

"Yeah. That's my friend Julie."

I finally walked over and gave my Aunt Geneva a proper kiss and hug. "It's great to see you," I said. "We've been having a lotta fun."

"I bet you have," she said, wiping Gino's forehead. "Why are you all so sweaty?"

"We've been playing basketball, Mom," Gino said. "Wanna see me shoot a basket?"

"Well, let me get situated. I've been driving in traffic for over two hours. Let me bring Aunt Lilly these pastries first."

"Later on, I'll show you how I can dive now," Gino said.

"That's news to me," I said flatly.

My mom finally popped out of the front door. "Geneva!"

"Hiya, Lil."

"I hope you're hungry and you brought a bathing suit in this heat," my mother said.

They embraced on the front porch while we all watched from the driveway.

"It might be too soon for me to swim," she said, "but maybe I'll get my feet wet."

And with that, the women walked into the house filled with sounds of barking dogs and the smell of a meat sauce slow-cooking on the stove.

Gino was hanging his head, so I suggested we all take a dip in the pool. While the girls all went to change, Gino and I went into the backyard and set up the rafts and the water guns we were going to use for what we had come to call the Godfather Game. It went like this: You jumped off the deck of the pool onto a giant raft and tried to recite lines of dialogue from the movie. All the while, you were getting shot at with high-powered water guns. And when you didn't make it across the thirty-two-foot pool, you had to stick the death scene just right and drop in the water as if you had just been whacked. And what made it easier was that my father had a thick book lying around the house called *The Mafia at War*, which had all the gory snapshots of the best rubouts of all time. We used it as a reference book.

My father was out back picking grapes from the arbor, with yellow jackets all over his arms.

"Daddy!" I said. "That's too many. You're gonna get stung!"

"Nah." He laughed. "How many years have you seen me do this? They're more afraid of us than we are of them."

"Jesus . . ." I said.

"Gino, did you hug and kiss your mother?" he asked.

"Yes," he said, and paused. "Uncle Al . . . ?"

"Yes?"

"You're not going to tell her about all those pills we buried, are you?"

My father stopped plucking grapes for a moment and shook the bees off his arms. "Hell no. A deal's a deal. I don't go back on my word. Go have fun in the pool."

With Gino and me playing in the pool with all the Rossitto girls, it wasn't long before Pete and his sister Tracy came by too. No one had fences back then. Everyone could see whatever their neighbors were up to.

Aunt Geneva sat in the kitchen with my mother and Aunt Mary, but her eyes seemed glued to the activities in the pool. I had slipped out for a few minutes and was sitting on a lawn chair outside the kitchen window.

"Lilly, what sort of game are they playing?" I heard Aunt Geneva say. "I see them shooting guns and the little girls act like they've been shot or something. Is that what I'm seeing?"

My mother and Aunt Mary laughed. "They play it every day. It's about *The Godfather*. They shoot each other with water guns like they're gangsters." My mother laughed.

"Has Gino seen *The Godfather* since he's been here?" she asked.

"Sure," my mother said nonchalantly. "Al took them a couple weeks ago."

"Oh God, no."

"What?" my mother said, clueless to my aunt's anxiety. "Was I supposed to call and ask you?"

"Lilly, a ten-year-old boy is not ready for that kind of violence."

My mother had a way of defusing things with a wave of her hand and also by walking away to tend to her sauce. "Well, Geneva, they saw it and they loved it. No harm done. It's a beautiful story about family."

"That's one way of looking at it. But it's not something I would have ever approved of," Aunt Geneva said to Aunt Mary, sitting across the table.

"Okay," my mother yelled out to the backyard, through every screen door and open window. "Sauce is done. I'm putting the pot up. Ten-minute warning!"

Those simple sentences, those arrangement of words, were a big type of structure in my life. With the meat sauce being slow-cooked since 10:00 a.m. and my mother telling two households that the pasta she was cooking would be ready to eat in ten minutes, that meant that all our loves and differences were about to be aired out at the big dining room table. And when she finally poured the macaroni into the *scolapasta* and the steam rose up all around her upper body and gathered at the framed portrait of Frank Sinatra above our sink, it was as close to religion as we ever got.

As we all gathered in the dining room and found our chairs, Gino began to tell his mother how much he enjoyed Aunt Mary's artwork. Whether it was a ceramics project or a clay sculpture or her tiny oil paintings inside giant, empty clamshells, Aunt Mary's work was fairly accomplished, despite the fact that she had been pretty much blind as a bat since birth. The unfortunate fact being, she was delivered while my grandmother had caught a case of syphilis on account of my grandfather stepping out one night too many. Anyhow, she never complained about it. Never even got mad at her father. She just decided it wasn't going to slow her down, and, as a result, she spent her life traveling the world, and her artwork was a testament to the things she could best remember that flashed before her eyes—a charging elephant in Africa, sunsets in South America, hula girls in Hawaii. Many of those sights got the large-canvas treatment, but a hundred more ended up delicately detailed on ordinary clamshells we dug out from the bay. And they were all over our house. It was like living with a far-sighted Dalí.

"Aunt Mary has been teaching me how to draw better," Gino said to his mother, holding up a drawing of a turkey that he had traced from his handprint.

"Well, look at that. I remember when you did the same thing when you were five or six years old," she said.

As my mother brought out the big pot of pasta and meat sauce, that comment took on a mean tone. And, as if on cue, her eyes met my father's at the same exact moment.

"Yeah, but Aunt Mary told me how to make it more special," Gino said. "She said to use my imagination so that the turkey can stand out from all the others."

Aunt Geneva grabbed his drawing and adjusted her glasses to get a better look. "Let me see," she said, as her jaw started to drop and her eyebrows furrowed. "Are these *pearls* around the turkey's neck?" she asked him.

"Yeah," Gino said with excitement. "A.J. drew his turkey with an Italian horn around its neck and high-top sneakers on its feet. I gave my turkey pearls."

"I see that. And it looks like you gave it high heels too," she said without any enthusiasm.

"Yeah. Isn't that funny? A boy turkey wearing pearls and high heels." Gino laughed, along with my sisters.

"I think it's hysterical," I said across the table.

"Why'd you stop there?" Aunt Geneva shot back. "Why not give him earrings?"

"That wouldn't look believable," my father piped up, as he sat in his chair at the head of the table. "Where would you hang 'em?"

Whether Aunt Geneva liked it or not, it became immediately apparent that my father—my whole family, in fact—accepted Gino's quirks without judgment. As a matter of fact, we began to celebrate them.

As usual, our table was overflowing with food. The meat sauce was just the start. And even though the sauce had meatballs, sausage, and braciola inside, that didn't mean my mother didn't also serve a London broil. And then there was always a big garden salad and some roasted peppers for good measure too. It was endless. As my mother and sisters began plating the food for all the men seated, my father was flipping through his albums, trying to find the right Sinatra song to go with the meal.

"Maybe we'll give Ol' Blue Eyes a break tonight," my father said. "I'm taking requests for dinner music. Anybody have anything they want to hear?

Lorraine was first to speak up. "Daddy, please play the *West Side Story* sound track."

"Hell no. Why? So you can hear Rita Moreno sing about wanting to live in America? Of course they want to live in America. We took them in and look where it got us. Every day there's another Puerto Rican murder in the papers."

"I guess the Jackson Five is out of the question?" I asked.

"No colored music," he mumbled. "Especially from the most fucked-up family in America. All of you will see one day. That family is just not right, and it starts with the father."

Aunt Geneva's cheeks were growing more red by the second. "Does this kind of talk go on all the time? My God, Al. Your language."

"It's nothing he hasn't heard before," my father said. "Or, if he wasn't hearing it . . . maybe he should have been."

"What's that supposed to mean?" Aunt Geneva said, pushing her plate aside.

With the grown-ups on full tilt, and everybody about to spill their guts about the one sensitive topic we were all biting our tongues over, it was Aunt Geneva who threw the first blow.

"I'm okay with no music at all during dinner," she said. "Dinner is a time for talking about your day, and I haven't seen Gino in many, many days."

It was impossible not to make eye contact with my entire family seated around me. And that comment was unfathomable for us. No one came to our house for quiet chitchat and casually catching up with each other. My house was a coliseum of emotions. And the dinner table had all the passion of an Italian opera. And you don't turn down the sound at the opera.

It didn't matter long, anyway, since my father paid Aunt Geneva's comment no mind and got back to work thumbing through his albums.

"Uncle Al . . . you know what I would really love to hear?" Gino said, quietly. "Do you have any Liza Minnelli records?"

I never remembered seeing any Liza Minnelli albums in the big green stereo console on those nights when my father was quizzing me on who were the world's "real" musicians, so I wasn't sure how he could make Gino's out-of-the-blue request come true.

"Ah, shit," my father said, genuinely disappointed, since Gino never asked for much. "I don't have any Liza here."

He turned to my sister Rosalie. "Ro, do you or Jack have any Liza at your house?"

Jack and Ro were a bit taken aback by the request and my father's true desire to make Gino's idea come to life. "No, Daddy," Ro said. "I'm sorry, Gino."

"Ah . . . it's okay," Gino said. "I just felt like hearing Liza."

My father was obviously intrigued. "How did you come to like Liza?" he said. "You know her mother, Judy Garland, was a real nut, right?"

"Yeah . . ." Aunt Geneva said. "Since when do you like Liza Minnelli? That's kind of random."

"Larry listens to her a lot," he told the table. "Sometimes he calls me in his room and plays her records and it helps me go to sleep. You remember, Mom?"

"I remember you falling asleep in Larry's room, yes," she said. "But I don't remember hearing the music."

And it was almost as if the memory of what his mother had just confirmed lifted his spirit right there at the dining room table. "I remember the music. I remember the words," Gino said. "I can still hear it in my dreams."

"Well, I'm sorry I can't get you Liza today," my father said. "But I think I have the next best thing right in here somewhere. Do you want to hear some of the songs from the man she was married to until a few weeks ago?"

There were a lot of men on album covers, so I had no idea which one of them might have been Liza Minnelli's former husband. I was just as confused as the rest of the table. I knew my father loved music and that he also had a fascination with all performers from the UK and Australia. He just thought that part of the world had a better sense of humor. But I didn't think his interest stretched into a song-and-dance man who wore sequined shirts with three buttons undone on the album sleeve.

"This is Peter Allen," my father said, holding up the record. "He's a helluva writer and a great performer. He's gonna be big."

"I've heard of him," both my sisters said.

"Well now listen to him."

The first song he dropped the needle on was "Tenterfield Saddler," as sad and syrupy as it gets, where Allen sings about his grandfather being an old, wise man who made saddles for people in a tiny Australian town, a father who found it easier to drink than go mad, and a little boy who grew up to marry a girl with a pretty face. Three generations of family delicately explained, whose dilemmas made ours seem like a walk in the park.

Gino was hooked immediately. "Wow, I *love* his accent," he said. "What else does he sing, Uncle Al?"

"Gino, dear, let Uncle Al eat," Aunt Geneva said.

"Forget it, Geneva," my mother countered. "He won't eat on Sundays until he finds the right music."

"Hey, Pop," Jack shouted, seeing that the room's usual stench of machismo was being compromised. "How about some Rolling Stones?"

"*Aspetta, aspetta.* This is more important."

Jack and Frankie both knew their place, and they were respectful to a fault. They quietly laughed across the table, seeing that there was an obvious shift taking place.

"Here, I found a beauty," my father said. "I can sit down and eat now."

The stereo played "Everything Old Is New Again," and as Gino listened, he developed a quiet ease about him. I knew my father always played with everyone's mind on a subliminal level, but it was more apparent than ever to me that the seeds he had planted a couple of months ago were finally giving way to a little sapling that was just beginning to get the right nourishment and light.

After dinner, Gino and I headed back into the pool to take another crack at finally teaching him to dive headfirst.

"Shouldn't you boys wait a half hour after you've digested dinner before you go back in the pool?" Aunt Geneva said.

"That's horseshit," my father told her. "Let them play. They're young boys. No one's gonna drown."

My mother and Aunt Geneva were seated across from each other at the kitchen table, having some coffee before my aunt headed back to Jersey. I was sitting in a giant black inner tube, and Gino, after a few more painful belly flops, had drifted off to sleep in an even bigger raft. He was one of those kids who could nod off anywhere, but drifting lazily in the shallow end of the pool was his favorite spot. He was like a cat that'd found a sun spot on the kitchen floor. And right about then the ladies got loud.

"Lil, I don't know how to say this, so I'm just going to say it," Aunt Geneva started.

"Say what, Geneva?" my mother said, at the same time motioning for Aunt Mary to leave the kitchen and head to the TV room.

"Well, I'm very thankful for you and Al being there for us. And allowing me time to recuperate. But, Lilly, I'm not sure I would've sent Gino here if I had known what he was getting into."

My father walked out the kitchen door, passed the pool,

and headed to see Jack and Ro. "Let them go at it," he told me. "It's overdue."

My mother grabbed her heart, pulling at her own shirt. "What the hell do you think he 'got into' over here?"

"I don't know where to start. . . ."

"Why don't you start with Larry's phone call, Geneva?" my mother said. "Your husband cried to us. He cried and you know why he cried. My heart still breaks from that night. But all we've done is given Gino support. So tell me what we're doing wrong."

"Oh, Lil," Aunt Geneva started. "The cursing, playing guns in the pool, and don't think I haven't seen the *Playboy* magazines in the bathroom. I just don't know what else to say. Isn't that enough? Forget about *my* son. . . . Aren't you worried about *your* son?"

"No, Geneva. I'm not worried about my son whatsoever," my mother said. "And the more you talk, the more hypocritical you sound. He was brought to us for a reason. Something, whatever it is, he wasn't getting. But he seems very, very happy this summer."

I quietly slid out of the pool, ran through the gate that separated our backyards, and poked my head in Rosalie's kitchen door. "Dad, it's getting bad in there. You guys gotta go break it up."

As I slid back into the pool, I heard the last few minutes before my father, Rosalie, and Jack entered the kitchen.

My mother was standing, her hands shaking too much to

light her own cigarette. "Maybe we didn't do what you *had* been doing. We didn't diagnose him. We just showed him love. He doesn't need medicine or a psychiatrist. This boy is wonderful."

My father didn't say a word—a first!—and let the women air it out.

"I'm sorry," my mother said. "I don't mean to say you and Larry don't show him love. I know you adore him."

"I know you didn't, Lil. I'm afraid I know exactly what you mean," she said.

"For chrissakes, Geneva, we're doing it the only way we've ever done it. Have you asked him how he feels about being here?"

"I know he loves his aunt Lil and uncle Al and everyone else," she said, tearing up. "It's hard on all of us. Please, let's not fight."

As Rosalie went to hug and kiss Aunt Geneva, my father put down the velvet hammer on it all. "Look, my brother called on me and we answered that call the best way we knew how. And here we are how many weeks later? Everybody is still alive, our kids are laughing, and life goes on."

As my mother and aunt embraced, I splashed Gino awake. "Hey, I think you're mom's getting ready to beat the traffic back home."

"How long was I asleep?" Gino asked.

"You didn't miss anything," I told him.

Before he climbed up the steps to kiss his mother good-bye, he turned away from me for a second. "This is gonna sound weird. But why am I still here, if my mother is healthy enough to be on her own at home?"

It's an answer I couldn't give him, other than to say we might as well finish out the summer together. "You got something better to do?"

"Umm . . . no, not really," he said.

That's when I laughed and pushed him back into the pool. "So quit worrying!"

15

ONE OF THESE NIGHTS

Now that both sets of our parents had gotten overemotional, at various times during the summer, the curiosity and intrigue had already filtered through my sisters and their partners and was now precisely dripping down on the foreheads of Gino and me. It was similar to the way we'd play Chinese water torture on a friend—hold them down on the ground and see how long they could take a single drop of water every five seconds or so. What starts out as fun and adventurous becomes maddening. I don't want to get overdramatic, but with Gino's stay coming to a close, there were some things I had to flush out and investigate for myself. And I was starting to feel fairly certain Gino was close to wanting to explain some things to me on his own.

The *Playboy* magazines I'd ended up getting my hands on were usually two or three months old. They arrived in the mail in my father's name, and my mother had no qualms handing him his new issue a few moments after he came home from work that particular night.

"Your *Playboy* came today," she would tell my father. And he would eat his dinner, down his liquor, and take my mother, the dogs, and the magazine upstairs to bed. And for the rest of the month, the *Playboy* would remain in his bathroom, alongside *National Geographic*, *Reader's Digest*, and *The Long Island Fisherman*, a flimsy newsprint guide that let anglers know where the fish were biting. Whenever the new *Playboy* arrived, the ritual would begin again, only at that point, I'd find him leaving the older *Playboy*s downstairs in different parts of the house. It was as if he wanted me to find them. And whenever five or six weeks had passed, I'd slip the *Playboy* upstairs to my room and stash it under my bed. It was a long-running ritual my father and I had. He'd never ask if anybody had seen last month's issue of *Playboy*, and I'd never take one out of his room before he'd brought it downstairs himself. There was a trust there. I'd also never do anything to mess with the magazine from its original state. No folding corners. Never getting the pages stuck together. Nothing like that. I stared and stared and stared at my favorite centerfolds, took care of my business, and expertly folded them back up and placed them beneath my mattress. They were like collectibles to me.

So you can imagine why I got a bit nuts when I reached for one, flipped the pages to my favorite face, and found a page torn out. The weird thing was, it wasn't even in the section of the magazine that featured naked women. It was a page way, way upfront, in the middle of the advertising section—the area that really frustrated young guys like me—and there was nothing on the preceding page that gave me any clue as to what sort of content was torn away.

Things were going nice and steady with Gino and me. We were in a good place, after his mom's visit had kind of figuratively whacked the wasps out of the hive. I came up on him one shitty, rainy afternoon—the kind of day that pounds you in the head and reminds you that beautiful, sunny Long Island summers sometimes come to an end very quickly in September.

He was lying in my bedroom, watching *Zoom* and singing along to its signature sing-off song:

Watch Zoom . . . Z, double O, M; Box three-five-oh;
    Boston, Mass. Oh-two-one-three-four. Send it to
    Zoom!

I opened the door to see him singing. "Oh . . . you missed a great episode," he told me.

"Yeah, I bet I did."

"That black girl you like, Zerena, was on a lot, like five times in three different segments," he said.

I shut off the TV and sat on the bed next to him. "You know what else I'm missing?" I asked.

"No."

"Here, let me show you," I said, reaching under the bed and grabbing the *Playboy* with the missing page. "I'm missing a page in this magazine. Do you know what happened to it?"

Gino began to act sheepishly, and his eyes wandered around the room, searching for an excuse.

"I know you *know*, cuz," I said. "No one else touched it. My *father* doesn't rip out pages in *Playboy*. Just tell me what you ripped out and why you did it."

"Well, don't get mad at me," he said.

"I ain't gonna get mad at you," I assured him. "Outside of me storming into the bathroom on you, has anyone in this house ever gotten mad at you?"

"No," he said softly.

"So, I just want to know why you ripped out the page. It's simple."

"Okay . . ."

"Just tell me, and I'll never ask you why again," I said.

"Well . . . it was a perfume ad, I think," Gino said.

"Perfume like my mother wears, or cologne like my father wears?" I said.

"No. Yes. It was a cologne picture."

I didn't like to see my cousin squirm, and because that moment seemed to be especially hard for him, I sort of let him off the hook. "I like some cologne ads too," I said. "Was it Canoe or Old Spice or one of those?"

Gino mustered up the bravery to reach under a pile of clothes and pull out the page. It was a dark-haired, blue-eyed man in an Old Spice ad. He was bare-chested, with a pretty blond girl draped behind him, erotically twisting around his body to smell his neck. The ad looked as though the couple either just had sex or were certainly about to. The guy was Mediterranean-handsome. The girl was a luscious-lipped blonde. The print read "Very convincing." Frankly, we both found an excuse to stare at the page, but for very different reasons.

Maybe it was all those episodes of *Columbo* I watched, I don't know, but I began to pull the truth out of Gino in a way that was more compassionate than coarse.

"It's cool," I said. "I can see why you like it."

"It is, right?" Gino said, opening up a bit.

"My father wears Old Spice, like, almost every day," I said. "Have you ever seen the TV commercials?"

"Yeah," Gino said, somewhat enthused. "But the guy in the magazine is different than the guy in the TV commercial. The guy on TV jumps off a boat and throws bottles of cologne at people wherever he goes. I think he's a sailor. And he's older than *this* guy."

"I know. The commercial has a guy in a navy peacoat," I said. "And the announcer says, 'Come on . . . wake up to the freshness of the open sea with Old Spice.'"

"Yeah, yeah." Gino laughed. "But all I know is, after this summer, the 'freshness of the open sea' smells like fish guts."

"And it also says . . . 'Feel the spray at your face and the wind at your back.'"

"Exactly," Gino said, thoroughly enjoying our bonding over the ad. My enthusiasm made him feel like he had done nothing wrong but rip out a page from an advertisement we both enjoyed.

But then my methodical interrogation began.

"So," I began, "did you look at the whole entire *Playboy* magazine before you ripped this page out?"

"Pretty much," he said.

"And you got past the girl in the middle, the centerfold, and everything . . . ?"

"Um, yeah," he said, somewhat surprised. "Because I remember the one centerfold said she wanted to be a veterinarian."

"Oh," I said, surprised. "You actually *read* the centerfold after you looked at it?"

"Well, yeah," he said.

"But you decided the pages of the naked girls should stay inside the magazine and the guy in the Old Spice ad needed to be ripped out?"

"Um . . . I guess, yeah."

"Are you pulling your pud to that guy?"

"What?" Gino said quizzically. "What are you even talking about?"

It was time for the good cop and bad cop in me to become one top cop.

I reached under the bed and pulled out several *Playboy* magazines. "Something ain't adding up," I said.

I laid out the magazines on the shag rug like a bounty. I opened up an iconic *Playboy* spread of Miss May 1974, Marilyn Lange, kneeling next to a kitten on top of a wicker chair. A page later she was actually pulling tufts of her pubic hair! Then I laid open Miss June 1974, Sandy Johnson, who stood there holding a Louisville Slugger fully nude except for a backward baseball cap, black cleats and knee-high athletic socks.

"What are you doing?" Gino said.

"Just, hold on," I said.

I reached deeper under my bed, behind the Candy Land box, and found dusty issues of Miss December 1973, Christine Maddox, a gorgeous California brunette who worked in a factory "putting little silver things on top of little plastic things," the article said. And, last but not least, I laid out a real collectible, Miss April 1973, the sexy, little black girl Julie Woodson.

"Just look at the pictures of all these girls," I said, a bit out of breath. "I don't understand why you would pull out a picture of the Old Spice guy and not one of these girls."

We got down on our knees and began to scan the layouts. Gino tried to pipe up ten seconds in. But I shut him up.

"Nope. Stop. Just look," I said. "*Really* look at the girls and tell me what happens to you."

After what seemed like five minutes of me turning pages in each magazine and even reading some copy from each of the centerfolds, I offered Gino the floor to speak.

"What do you want me to say?" he said.

"Do any of these naked girls have any effect on you?" I said. "Do they, at least, make your dick hard?"

"No," he said. "That doesn't . . . oh my God . . . I just . . . no." He kind of rolled his eyeballs.

"How the hell could that be?" I said. "Just look."

"I am."

"No. Look *longer*," I said.

"I have," Gino said. "I am."

"No. Look at Miss June's big tits," I said, tapping the magazine quite hard. "Look at how hot Miss May looks touching her beaver hair."

"I'm looking."

"Look. Julie Woodson," I pleaded. "Have you ever *seen* a naked, black girl?"

"No, I haven't," he said softly. "But I don't care."

I sat there next to him on the rug, flustered and emotionally exhausted. I had nowhere else to go.

"Then what is it? What? Is it because you're just ten years old?" I offered. "Gimme something to work with here."

"No. I don't know," he started. "I know . . . I see the girls are all beautiful. It just . . . doesn't matter to me."

"Okay," I said. "I'm not gonna get mad. Just try and tell me why."

Gino got up and sank facedown into the bed. He acted like he had just finished a prizefight. "It's because I'm *different*," he said. "I don't understand it, and I know you can't understand it—and my parents don't understand it—but I'd rather look at the men in the magazine."

While Gino spoke facedown, and his words bounced off the wall he was facing, I was lying on the carpet, flat on my back amid all the girls—the very artillery I assumed would render him weak and able to see things my way. But I whiffed. It all went to shit. My greatest plan, which I had been plotting for some time, was rendered useless within minutes.

After a long pause, and a lot of reflective thought on my part, I quietly asked Gino a serious question. "Is that why you liked having Nolan around? On the boat and in the movie theater?"

"Pretty much," Gino said. "He was always a grown-up who just listened to me and, you know, didn't think I was weird or anything."

"So, you had a crush on him or something?"

Gino waited a few seconds to answer. "Remember, you said you wouldn't get mad at me whatever I told you. . . ."

"Yeah, yeah," I said. "I ain't mad."

"So . . . well, yeah, I guess I did have a crush on him or something," he said, sitting up in the bed. "He listened to me and was sweet and gentle. There wasn't anything wrong with it. He was just a nice guy."

My mother called up from the foot of the stairs, telling us dinner was on the table, kind of shocking me back to reality.

"You're right," I said, carefully scooping up the *Playboy*s and sliding them back beneath my bed. "I don't understand, man. I'm trying. But I really don't completely understand."

A few minutes later, at the dinner table, my mother picked up on a difference between us—maybe it was posture or attitude, who knows? But she had no qualms letting us know she was hip to something being off between my cousin and me. "What the hell's wrong with you two?" she said. "You both look like *who* did it and *why*."

"Nothing," I said, ignoring her intuitive probe. "What did you make for food?"

"Tacos," she said, with a hefty confidence.

"What the hell are *tacos*?" I said, as Gino and Lorraine laughed into their hands. "Thursdays are usually meat loaf. What happened?"

"It's the same thing. Chop meat is chop meat and I decided to try tacos," she told us.

"Oh Jesus." I huffed.

"What did you say?"

"Nothing, Ma. Just . . . don't know why you wanna surprise us out of nowhere. Why do people want to surprise people?" I said. "I just really look forward to eating meat loaf."

"Well, talk to your sister," she said. "Lorraine said she's getting sick of it."

I sat down next to my smirking sister and whispered, "Whatever happens is your *damn* fault."

As my mother pulled the hot taco shells from the oven and laid out the ingredients on the table—spicy chopped meat, diced tomatoes, sliced bits of cheddar cheese, tiny strings of lettuce, sour cream, and salsa—she began telling us in which order the fixings were to be applied.

We began to all get exasperated. It felt more like an art project than dinner. The taco shells were breaking in our hands, salsa was running down our chins, and Lorraine and I had some pointed advice for our mother's failed attempt at Mexican cuisine. "I don't know how to say this," Lorraine said, "but the lettuce is too *cold*. Does that make sense?"

"Yeah," I said. "And the meat is too hot. And the sour cream is too runny. It's too many different temperatures at once, Ma."

Gino broke his shells apart and just ate the meat with his fork.

"You too?" my mother said to Gino.

"I'm sorry, Aunt Lilly. It's not something I've ever eaten."

"And it's something she's never made," I said. "So don't feel too bad. Does Daddy know you made *Mexican* food?"

"Ah . . . go shit in your hat," my mother told all of us. "I'll worry about your father. There's cereal in the cabinet if you're hungry." She walked away to put her feet up in her chair and watch the news.

Later that night, we kind of kept to ourselves. Gino visited the Rossitto girls and played some sort of a séance game, and I stayed at home and made some lead fishing weights in the garage with Jack and Frankie. I could hear the whole lot of them laughing in the backyard, but it just felt better being with the men for a change.

I hit the sack pretty early afterward, with me falling asleep before Gino even got home from next door. I think the pressure of the day, and the fact that I still hadn't cracked the code, had gotten the best of me. As I awoke the next morning, the sun was shining bright again, and I immediately began hoping for an Indian summer. I hadn't even yet thought of what had earlier occurred in my bedroom between two cousins and four *Playboy* magazines. I was still in those precious first few seconds of being awake before the events of the prior day have a chance to sneak up behind me and slam into the back of my head. Just then, I could make out the soft sounds of Gino singing in the shower. It wouldn't have bugged me except for the fact that I had heard him sing this particular song nearly all summer long. And on that day, I had just had enough.

I got out of bed and crept to the bathroom door, and as I got closer I could make out the words to a song that I'd always felt was nothing short of a real downer. I mean, there wasn't any way I could apply the words to my life. I found it confounding why Gino was so attached to it. It made me want to scream.

Once again, I pressed the tip of my fingernail into the lock, sneaked into the bathroom, and just knelt down against the wall and listened to the sounds of shower water gently pelting the plastic curtain, the *squish* and overpowering smell of the Herbal Essences shampoo, the squeaky feet on the tub, and, of course, Gino's high-pitched singing. But try as I might, as I heard Gino sing several minutes of Maureen McGovern's sad song about a luxury liner getting hit by a tsunami on its final voyage from New York City to Greece on New Year's Eve, I couldn't hold myself back from reacting like a madman.

I hollered over the water, "Jesus Christ, Gino, why are you always singing 'The Poseidon Adventure'?"

After he let out a bit of a shriek, he calmly answered me. "It's called 'The Morning After.'"

"Same fuckin' thing."

It wasn't like he even knew the whole song. I hated Maureen McGovern as much as I hated the miserable song and its morbid message. But at *least* I knew every word. Gino would just sing the beginning with all his heart, before humming the rest: "There's got to be a morning after, if we can hold on through the night. We have a chance to find the sunshine. Let's keep on looking for the light. Humm, hmm hmm hmm hummm hmm hmm, hmm, hummm."

If I heard it once that summer, I heard it a thousand times.

"What is it with you and that song?" I demanded. "What is it about that *one* song that you're always either singing it or humming it whenever you're all alone?"

Gino shut off the water, pulled a towel from the rod, and asked me to give him a couple of minutes. And, honestly, after the summer he'd been through, he'd at least earned that. I shut my mouth and slid back down the wall until I was squatting on the floor in the foggy bathroom as I let him compose himself. Then Gino laid down some heavy shit for a ten-year-old.

"Can I put on some underwear and shorts first?" he asked me.

"Yeah," I said, exhausted. "Just do whatever you gotta do. But just . . . enough bullshit. Tell me what's up."

Gino leaned against the sink, crossed his arms, and let go. Once again, his eyes began to tear. But this wasn't about any allergies he might have suffered from.

"Okay. There is a part of me that hates being a kid and always feeling nervous about things," he said. "I can't explain it, A.J., but there's something in that song that makes me feel good. That maybe someday things will be easier for me."

"Just try and tell me why you feel like you're on a sinking ship," I begged. "I saw the movie. People died. People were saved. It was crazy. I'm sick of the song, but what does it do for you?"

"Well, I guess it's the part about being saved," he said. "I hear the song and I just think somebody will understand how I feel someday." At this point he was flat out crying.

"Do you think everyone thinks you don't fit in . . . something like that?" I said.

He coughed out a laugh. "I *don't* fit in. Even I know that," Gino said. "I'm not sure if I ever will. I've felt this way for a while."

"Okay, look," I said. "I'm sorry I barged in *again*. Listen . . . we're cousins and we love each other. I don't understand everything, but I see how this 'fitting in' thing is killing you. So . . . I'm gonna back off, okay?"

"Okay," Gino said, wiping off.

"You cried when you first got here," I said. "But I don't want you bawling on the way out."

"Trust me," Gino said. "I don't wanna sing that song all the time, it just makes me feel good, is all."

I got up off the floor and wrapped my arms around Gino's wet head. "I gotta ask you one question though," I said.

"Okay . . ."

"Who would you rather be on that boat, Gene Hackman or Shelley Winters?"

"Oh," he said. "Shelley Winters. But then, I *always* want to be Shelley Winters!"

16

WHATCHA SEE IS WHATCHA GET

By the time September had rolled in, my father had finally acquiesced and allowed me to play Pop Warner football. Ever since kindergarten I could remember that almost every kid in the neighborhood was playing some sort of sport—mainly Little League baseball and, to a lesser extent, basketball. But football was religion in my little town—with practices running so late that fruit bats would make dives at our white helmets after dark. The coaches acted like they didn't see anything, and none of the parents ever complained, as far as I can remember.

Since that summer was my first year at playing any kind of organized sport, I had some problems fitting in. It's not that I wasn't any good. Hell, I could outrun almost everyone on the Golden Bears, Marauders, Pirates, and Red Raiders. The problem was, I hadn't been doing the drills, hitting the dummies on the fields, and attending the pizza parties with the same group of kids and coaches for the last seven years, so I didn't become part of the in-crowd. And that was something my father alluded to when I first asked about joining. My father had been a football and track star in high school, but he didn't grow up with any sort of league. In his day, you played in the streets until you were ready for the school yard. He never told me as much, but I'd always felt that with his working late six days a week—and also being a good twenty-five years older than the other fathers and coaches on the field and in the bleachers—the politics of it all would end up biting me in the ass. And there'd be little he could do to protect my ego.

But with Jack in his ear, constantly begging him to get me into football before I entered junior high school—"Pop, listen to me, we *gotta* get him on their radar"—he began to weaken his stance. That change was hard on all of us. Jack and Ro would end up dropping me off and picking me up from practices, and every Sunday my father would put off fishing to come see my games—which were jam-packed with half-drunk dads and flirty moms—much to the shame of a lot of the kids who were out there playing in pads. But my father was right. The teams were filled with cliques of kids and coaches and ass-kissing parents all around. But we stuck it out. I was never the best on the team, but in time I figured out how to be accepted and admired and get my ass into the game. Most important, I never embarrassed myself. Even to the extent that I was the first kid to accept a dare from my coach and former marine, Mr. John Nicholson, who wouldn't answer to anything but Special Sergeant. He was something else, that guy. He made us sing the marine hymn to and from games and at the end of every practice. One Sunday, we had a special road game planned against a team way out in East Orange, New Jersey, in which we were going to sleep over at the houses of the players we were pitted against. Coach Nicholson demanded to know if any of us boys had the balls to pee on their lawns at night and, further, gain entry into the opposing player's mom and dad's bedroom and smack a USMC sticker beneath the mom's pillow.

"This mission will not be an easy one," Nicholson said, smoking a cigarette and chewing gum. "Life is gonna put obstacles in your path. You're job is to evaluate and overcome. But if you can do this, you can do anything life throws at you."

I shot my hand up first. "I'll do it," I said. "Just gimme the sticker and it's done."

And that's just what I did a couple of nights later, when I excused myself from a game of Scrabble with the wonderful and accommodating Pacifico family, and sneaked into their master bedroom and stuck the decal on the bottom of a pillow and calmly walked back to the board game. I told Nicholson my mission was accomplished on the morning of the game. He leaned over and kissed my helmet, then started me at right end.

"That's one helluva boy you got there, Al," he shouted to my dad during kickoff.

My father seemed proudest of that moment.

It was understandable why Gino never really wanted to go watch me practice as his stay with us was coming to an end. We played at the Beach Fields, which was a nice little park built about two hundred yards in from the beaches of the Great South Bay. Most practices went for three hours in ninety-degree heat, with as many mosquitoes running rampant as there were hormones raging. Every huddle had an argument, every play from scrimmage featured a coach grabbing us by our face masks and disciplining us in some ways that would undoubtedly make the nightly news nowadays. Not to mention, when we did get one of our two "mandatory" water breaks, we all lined up and sucked from the same filthy garden hose.

The one saving grace was knowing that my sister Rosalie would be there to pick me up in her yellow Chevy Nova. Of course, when it came to Ro, there was always a small price to pay for her patiently waiting for practice to end. She always worked an angle. Especially on Wednesday nights, since Thursday morning was when the sanitation workers were scheduled to haul away people's trash. Not stinky kitchen garbage, mind you. Trash. Trash had value. Trash meant other people's treasure, like furniture, televisions, bicycles, picnic tables, et cetera. And since we could get a jump on what some folks were going to leave at the curb on Wednesday nights, Rosalie was all-in on the action. Problem was, I wasn't.

It didn't matter to me that my sister was one of the original Dumpster divers, and on many occasions she'd surface with something of value. What mattered was that we were sometimes pulling up to houses of my classmates, who had no trouble spotting me in the passenger seat, while my sister rummaged through their junk.

"Ro, can we just go straight home tonight, please?" I begged, sweating like a pig and still wearing full pads.

"I just have to drive down Duck Lane," she said. "I'm gonna need your help with what I think was a beautiful, wrought-iron standing lamp."

"Oh Jesus, no."

And it never ended with Duck Lane. Once she had me in the car, there was no telling what wealthy neighborhoods she'd drive through. And I'd have to suffer the indignity of maybe seeing a cute girl I liked, while my sister had me help her cram rattan chairs, stained-glass windows, or television sets that looked to be fine. And for the really big scores that we couldn't stuff inside the car, she always carried rope so that we could tie another man's trash to the roof of her car and leave the scene without any dignity intact at all. That's a big reason why I believed Renee Schneider never went on a movie date with me. One Wednesday night she saw me in full football gear, tying a fish tank stand to the roof of the car. First impressions are everything.

Once we had our car literally stuffed with other men's junk, my embarrassment subsided and I had to cut Ro in on the conversations and altercations I had been having with Gino. "Take the long way home," I told her. "I gotta talk to you about Gino."

Rosalie stared straight ahead at the road but patted my thigh and kind of smirked. "I know you do," she said. "You have questions you want to ask me, right?"

"You ain't kiddin'," I said.

If she wasn't so good spotting a bargain in a trash heap, my sister could've had a long career as a prosecuting attorney. Like most problems or family squabbles that came her way, she was always ready and had the answers prior to your questions even being asked.

"Do you remember the day Gino was coming to see us and you were driving Mommy crazy with all your talk about 'brain damage'?" she said.

"Those weren't my words, Ro. That's what Uncle Larry, Daddy, and Mommy said."

"I know, I know," she said, wiping my sweaty head. "They put those stupid words in your head."

"Thank you."

"But the first thing I told you, 'Gino isn't as rough a boy as you are. Wasn't as tough a boy as you are.' Do you remember that?"

"Kinda," I said, searching in my cluttered brain. "But there was so much shit going on that day, I don't know what I remember anymore."

"Well, that's what I told you. I don't forget what I say. And I don't lie to you."

"Pull over," I asked her. "We're almost home and I'm not done yet with something."

She pulled the car to the side, as the junk inside the car and on the top slid forward a little.

"Ro," I began. "The other day we were looking at *Playboy*s and Gino told me he liked looking at the men more than the girls. It was an Old Spice ad and he just flat out said that he knew the girl was pretty, but it was the man he liked looking at more."

"Okaaay . . ."

"And I always catch him sobbing and singing that *Poseidon Adventure* song in the shower. The last morning I finally walked into the bathroom and had to find out what is it about that song that he's always singing it, ya know?"

"Yeah. Oh, how I hate that depressing song," she said.

"That's what I'm saying, Ro. We all hate that song, but he said it makes him feel like one day things will be different for him and easier or—and these are his exact words—like he'll be *saved*."

"Aww, that's sad," she said. "Did you get mad at him?"

"No," I said. "I just calmed him down and promised him I wouldn't bring it up anymore."

"You're a good cousin, A.J.," she told me. "A lot of boys would've had a hard time with that."

There were a few seconds of silence in the car as Rosalie let all the emotional dust settle.

"What do you think Gino is trying to tell you? What do you think is so hard for him to talk about in his life?" Ro said.

"That he doesn't like girls."

Rosalie then asked me if that, at all, bothered me.

"Nah," I said. "But it seems really tough on him."

Rosalie started up the car again and slowly merged back onto the road. "I know this is hard for you to understand now. It's hard for a lot of people to understand, especially Gino," she said. "Daddy and Uncle Larry are from a different generation. Trust me, Gino will have an easier time of it as the years go by, just like his brother, Larry, did."

"I hope so," I said. "I wish they'd stop calling it 'brain damage.' Because it ain't."

"You're right," she said. "Sometimes people mean well but say the wrong things."

When Rosalie and I got home, she helped remove my jersey and shoulder pads before we called out to anybody who might have been home.

"Ma . . . we're home," Rosalie hollered. When nobody answered back, we slowly followed the bit of a ruckus we heard going on in the kitchen. The room sounded like it had more than just my mother and Gino inside it.

"They didn't hear us," Ro said.

"Let's see what's going on."

When we entered the room I saw what looked like the

early stages of a pajama party unfolding right there at my kitchen table. Standing in a half circle, with their backs to us, were Lorraine, Arlene, Aunt Mary, Aunt Mae, and my cousin Grace Marie. In other words, a typical summer night.

"Hello," Ro said. But nobody turned around.

When we finally walked to the table and into the thick of the action, the girls parted and revealed my mother sitting on a spinning kitchen chair with enough metal on her head to look like a human satellite. It wasn't until I got right on them that I saw Gino combing the sides of her hair and making room for more.

"What the hell is going on?" I shrieked, looking at all the happy and amused female faces.

"Gino is curling my hair," my mother calmly said.

"I can see that," I said. "With what?"

"Soda cans," the girls all said, and laughed.

Apparently, while I was slaving away at practice (and climbing through neighbors' trash), Gino had suggested a get-together for all the women. "Some of my electric rollers were broken," Lorraine turned to me and said, with a head full of loose curls. "So Gino told us he could do a better job with Coke cans."

"You gotta be kidding me," I said. "Where the hell did you learn how to do that?"

"I've seen my brother Larry do my sisters' hair a hundred times," Gino said.

I turned to Rosalie a few feet behind me. "What do you

say about that?" I said. Rosalie handed me her pocketbook and walked into the fray. "I'm next!" she said.

When I finally accepted what was happening, I was able to focus in on the table that was stacked with empty soda cans of Tab, Fresca, Shasta, White Rock, Dad's, and plenty of Cokes. In addition, Arlene, Grace Marie, and Lorraine had all brought their nail polish kits too. Apparently, the girls who weren't sitting in the curling chair at "Chez Gino" were all passing the time by coloring their nails.

"Gino," my mother joked, "what can you do with A.J.'s mop?"

"Yeah, right," I said. "How much longer until you're all done taking over the kitchen?"

"That depends how long it takes Gino to give me fuller hair with more volume," Rosalie laughed.

After my mother told Ro to wash her hair in the sink, Gino explained to me how easy it was—"Practically a snap," he said—to use soda cans instead of curlers. With my mother's hair finally set, Gino used Rosalie's wet hair to explain: "First you give a real good comb-out," he said. "Then you part the hair in the middle and clip the sides out of the way."

"Oh, Gino," Lorraine said. "You sound like a real hairdresser in a fancy salon."

"Oh my God . . ." I said.

"Then you start in the middle, from the top of the head to the back," Gino continued, grabbing a Fresca can and wrapping her hair around it. Then he kept it in place with a rubber band before he moved on to the next curl and can. "It's easy, A.J." He giggled. "You could even do this. It's a lot easier than diving." That got a good laugh from all the girls. And it got me to walk away, take a long, hot shower, and clear my head.

When I dried off and went back downstairs, I saw that the party in the kitchen had ended and a small group had assembled by the steps of the pool. On warm summer nights the best relief from the heat and humidity was taking a late dip in the pool with all the citronella candles lit and the light in the deep end perfectly illuminating the pool so that you could see all the dents our heels made in the mushy vinyl at the bottom. Before I pushed through the dining room screen door and dived into the pool, I hung back to watch what looked like a tender scene unfolding in the shallow end. Rosalie was on the steps of the pool. She was holding her son, my two-year old nephew, Jackie. He was fearless of the water and loved to walk to the third step, where the water was up higher than his diaper. I watched as Jackie cackled at his accomplishment and his chest heaved with excitement at the cool temperature of the water and the gentle splashes that shot up and rained down to rest on his curls.

Then my mother, even with a mountain of soda cans still on her head, looked so elegant as she softly swam up to Gino on the steps and pulled him in close against her favorite flower-patterned one-piece. If my father had a way of realigning the gravitational pull of the entire day if he raised his voice

to the right level, my mother's nuances and quiet encouragement could change your outlook on life in no time at all.

"How is my beautiful nephew?" she said softly into Gino's
ear. "Thank you so much for my beauty parlor treatment.
Oh . . . you spoiled me!"

Gino blushed a little as he pushed off to meet her at the
foot of the steps. "Oh . . . you're welcome, Aunt Lilly. I was
happy I could do that for you."

"You know something? I saw your face on the first day
you got here and your aunt Lilly could tell, I don't think you
had any idea what the hell you were getting yourself into, did
you?"

"Yeah. No," Gino said. "I really didn't know. Especially
after those first few days!"

"Well," my mother went on, "those two can be real ball-
breakers—my husband and my son. But they only wanted
what was best for you, honey. You know that, right?"

"Yeah. I know."

"But, listen to me, sometimes Frick and Frack are more
bark than bite. I wish they wouldn't yell so loud and get so
goddamn passionate about everything. I mean, my son thinks
he's the policeman of the world! I know you know what I'm
talking about."

"Yeah," Gino said. "I think I know what you mean."

The two of them shared a laugh and floated across to the
other side of the shallow end, closest to where I was standing—hiding behind the dining room's screen door.

"Well, you might have heard your mother and I getting a little loud the other day," she said.

Gino cocked his head and leaned in a bit closer as my mother lowered her voice to a whisper.

"Let me tell you something, your mother and your father love you very, very much. You know that."

"Umm-hmm," Gino said, staring down at the water.

"But sometimes it's not so easy raising a young boy at different times in his life. You know your cousin A.J., he was a real friggin' project, let me tell you."

"A.J. was, huh?" Gino laughed.

"Oh my God. Last year we didn't know if he'd finish the fifth grade," she said. "He was a bundle of nerves, full of twitches and stomachaches, and we didn't know what the hell to do with him."

"I didn't know anything about that," Gino said, slightly smiling. "He acts like he's always together and everything."

"Ha!" My mother laughed. "Your uncle Al and I were pulling our hair out—'What are we gonna do with this kid?'"

"What'd you do?"

"Well, we just asked for help, Gino," she said. "We went to Aunt Mae, Arlene, Ro, Jack, NuNu, and Frankie, anyone we could think of. And little by little, with everybody pitching in here and there, we got him on his feet and past a very, very tough time for him."

"What do you think was wrong with him?" Gino asked softly.

"Sometimes boys have a rough go of it, you know? It has to do with how old you are, who your friends are, if your family is listening to you. Don't you feel that way sometimes?"

"Well, yeah, but I didn't think A.J. got that way," Gino said.

"Let me tell you, boy oh boy, was your cousin on the ropes! He didn't know if he was coming or going."

"And he's better now?"

"I think so, yeah," she said. "But it doesn't mean he won't need help down the road one day. Everybody needs a little help getting through life every now and then. And I think your mother and father brought you to us at the perfect time in all of our lives."

"Yeah, Aunt Lil, that makes sense," he said.

"Are you happy you're here, or are you ready to go home?"

"Well, I love being here. But I do miss seeing everybody at home," Gino said. "I'm anxious to tell them how much fun I had. How I learned to clam and catch crabs and kill slugs and grab earthworms . . ."

I broke up the warm embrace my mother and Gino were sharing by sticking my head out the door and finishing his sentence. "But you still can't dive!"

"No," Gino yelled to me. "I'm doing that too. Watch!"

He gently pushed his way past Rosalie and Jackie and bounced up the steps. Then he streaked past me on the white concrete slabs that separated the house from the pool before jumping onto the diving board in the deep end. He came to a complete stop at the very edge and let out a nervous giggle. "A.J., I'm gonna do this," he said defiantly.

"Then do it," I said. "Just bend your knees, squeeze your ears, and lean forward."

I remember I held my breath the exact moment I saw Gino do the same. But this time when he bent his body forward, there was no moment of panic or hesitation as he got into position. He shot the water a look of determination and began a slow push forward that meant as much to him as it did for me. I watched Gino slice into the still water and perfectly dive into the pool without so much as a splash as his body slipped underneath. I'm sure he could hear all our cheers eight feet down. It looked like a baptism of sorts, where he was washing away some of the summer's shame, the frustration, and especially the unknown. I always said being in water made that boy feel equal on some sort of other level.

17

SHINING STAR

At some point, I grabbed a calendar off the wall and started doing some math. I'm not sure if it was because I was keyed up that my first year of junior high school was approaching or disappointed that summer was coming to a close. It could have even been I was just plain curious about what the coming days would be like without Gino by my side. I flipped a few pages, did some quick math, and saw that Gino had been with us for almost an entire summer vacation. Labor Day was a week away, and I knew Uncle Larry was set to pick him up and whisk him back to Jersey that weekend. I was a little uneasy with that. There was no way around it: I was gonna miss having him around.

Normally, whenever a relative or close friend had spent any extended time with us, it was customary to throw some sort of going-away dinner for them. Nothing too huge, mind you. But, in addition to the usual big dinners my mother cooked up, we always carved out time to make a cake or a big fat *pizza rustica* pie the day the person was leaving. I'm not sure when that started, but I don't remember a time when that didn't exist. Hell, we never needed any excuses to eat more food or have more fun around the table anyway. But then it was the Friday before the holiday and I hadn't heard a thing about anybody doing anything special for Gino's departure.

I quietly approached my mother while she was busy paying some bills at the kitchen table. That was always a delicate time because she never used a calculator and we never had enough money.

"Ma, what are you doing?"

"Bouncing checks left and right," she said. "What's the matter?"

"Uncle Larry's coming to get Gino on Sunday, right?"

"No. He called. He's gotta work Sunday," she said, licking her fingers to turn the pages of the checkbook. "So he's coming tomorrow."

"*Tomorrow!*"

"Yeah, tomorrow morning," she said. "What's the problem?"

"Well, it's just that Gino's been here, like, eighty days . . ."

"What'd you look at, a calendar?"

"No, really, Ma. It's about eighty days, give or take," I explained. "Are we, uh, doing something for him?"

"What do you want me to do? We opened our door for your cousin for the whole summer. You want me to bake a cake too?"

"Well, yeah," I said. "Some kind of big dinner or cake or something. You know, like we usually do."

She sat up in her chair and spun the checkbook at me. "Here, look," she said. "If a trip around the world cost five dollars, we wouldn't have enough money to get off the block!"

"Come on, Ma, I'm serious," I said as she gave me a look. "Well, then, what are you making for dinner tonight?"

"Your father feels like tuna fish," she said.

"*Tuna fish!* That's not even *cooking*. What's wrong?"

"If you don't want tuna fish, I got peppers and eggs," she said, folding the checkbook closed. "We never eat meat on Fridays."

"Can't we make an exception?" I begged. "Who the hell are we kidding? We're not even religious."

"Watch your mouth," she said, lighting a cigarette and walking out of the room. "Tuna or eggs. You'll live."

It wasn't like my mother to be so matter-of-fact on the subject of dinner, but I said all I could on the matter. Outside of appealing to Lorraine and Ro, there was little I could do. I was more disappointed in what Gino would feel come dinnertime. Not that he was a huge eater or anything, but even he would know such simple dishes were not the norm for our family. Especially on the eve of his leaving. Still, I couldn't resist running upstairs to our bedroom and pulling his attention away from PBS.

"For some reason, all we're having is tuna fish for dinner tonight," I said.

"Okay," Gino said.

"That's all," I said. "No fish, no cutlets, no pasta, nothing."

"That's fine. With me packing and all, I don't think I'm gonna have a huge appetite anyhow."

"Did you know you were leaving *tomorrow* and not Sunday?"

"Yeah, my father has to work Sunday, so he called this morning and said he's coming tomorrow." He went back to watching TV.

"And you're okay with that on such short notice?" I said.

"Yeah, I guess. What can I do about it?"

"*Jesus*, what's wrong with everybody?" I said.

It took up a big part of the day, but eventually I simmered down and tried my best to make Gino's final full day somewhat memorable. We spent the afternoon shooting baskets at the hoop before a dozen or so friends wandered over to play ball and say good-bye to Gino. That's the way it was growing up in a new development of homes back in the 1970s. I don't recall any summer day when I wasn't a part of ten to fifteen boys looking for some hell to raise. It wasn't like that for Gino back in Succasunna. And as the summer wore on, he became as spoiled as I was, literally acting bratty or disappointed whenever a dozen or so friends didn't materialize within a half hour of us walking outside the front door.

"Don't look now," he said, "but here comes Coogan."

"Okay. Don't worry about anything, I'll handle it," I said.

Gino wasn't sweating it too much, but he couldn't help but wonder why Coogan was headed for us with a smirk on his face after what went down in his foyer earlier that summer.

"You think he'll start anything?" he asked.

"After the scene my father made, he'd have to be out of his mind to even think about it."

We braced ourselves for the worst, until it was clear that all Coogan wanted to do was fall back in good graces of us. "Hey, man," he shouted from the sidewalk. "Lemme take a half-court shot."

"You suck from out there," I said as I rolled him the ball.

Gino and I followed the arc of his shot and watched it clank off the top of the backboard. "*Brick*," I shouted as Gino laughed to himself.

"Big whoop, I hate basketball anyway," Coogan said.

To Gino's credit, he ran to fetch the ball, and Coogan followed him before finally addressing him for the first time. "Hey, man, how much longer are you gonna be here?" he asked.

When Gino explained he was leaving the next day and that tonight was actually his final night, Coogan looked a bit depressed. "No shit? I was gonna invite you guys to go fishing for bluefish on our boat Sunday."

"Really?" I said. "How does your dad feel about that?"

"It was his idea," he said. And then his expression gave way to the real embarrassment he was feeling. "Dude," he said to Gino. "It was my brothers' idea, that whole sidewalk thing. I didn't want any part of it. They're too scared to come by and apologize to your face. But I will for them."

For some reason, I never felt comfortable watching a guilty party grovel and apologize for some dumb thing they had done. I felt my father's anger was enough to even the score. Listening to a heartfelt apology made me squirm.

"It's cool, Coogan," I said, kind of cutting him off. "It's in the past. I didn't think that was something you dreamed up."

And just when I was willing to let it go away, Gino spoke up. "Yeah, A.J. said he knew it had to be your dumb brothers anyway, because you probably know how to spell *queer*."

That comment left me happily stunned, but it also melted Coogan into a bundle of awkward expressions and forced laughter. "Hey, you're okay with me, Gino," he said. "Sorry you're leaving now that we're finally getting to know each other. But I'm sure we'll hang out more the next time you visit."

"Yeah, he'll be coming more often from now on," I said.

After a few minutes more of shooting hoops and playing several games of H-O-R-S-E, Pete D'Ascoli and Richie Tischler spilled out of Pete's garage and raced their new skateboards up and down my driveway.

"There they are . . . the Benza boys!" Peter hollered. "What are we doing today?"

Gino looked at me, a bit overwhelmed with his warm greeting. "I don't know," I said. "What do you guys wanna do?"

"Well, I sure as hell don't think Gino wants to play kickball, do you, Gino?" Richie deadpanned.

"Yeah, um, no thanks." Gino nervously laughed.

When the Rossitto family ran out of their house, looking to join in the fun, I felt it was necessary to tell everyone about Gino's sudden exit plan.

"This is Gino's last night," I said out loud. "He leaves tomorrow morning. For good."

"For good, like *forever* for good?" Pete said.

"No, man. Just for this summer. He starts school next week like we do," I said.

Pete and Richie hopped off their boards and began throwing shadow punches at Gino's midsection. "Well, that sucks," Pete said. "I was just getting used to you always being around."

"Yeah, and I was starting to think maybe not everyone from New Jersey is a douche bag." Richie laughed as he mocked pulling his junk out of his zipper. "You're cool with me, *WEE*-no."

"It's Gi-NO, Richie *TIT*ler," Gino said.

As the bunch of us laughed, Richie quickly folded up Gino's body and playfully pinned him to the grass. Maybe my cousin didn't know it at the time, but I remember thinking that's as close as he's ever going to get to those guys showing their love and respect toward him. However awkward and trying the past two and a half months had been, it was all melting away under the early-evening sun on my front yard.

Before the group of us could put together any kind of organized plans for a fun-filled last night, my father's car raced down the block and turned into the driveway as all us kids scattered to different parts of the porch.

"Hey, it's Uncle Al the kiddie's pal," Richie shouted.

My father rolled out of his Mustang while tucking a conspicuous shopping bag under his left arm. He then called for Pete to pass him the basketball before tossing a one-handed hook shot right through the net from thirty feet away on the lawn.

"Up your ass from the grass," he said, while marching into the house and kissing my mother in the foyer. A few seconds later, she appeared before the screen door and told Gino and me to get ready to wash up and have dinner with the family.

I said good-bye to the gang before turning to Gino. "Some friggin' dinner," I said.

After we were done washing up, Gino and I went back to our room, where I gave him a little hand putting things away in his luggage. He was kind of quiet, even when I joked that I wanted to stash a *Playboy* magazine in his bag. But I did manage to tell him how happy I was to see him finally turn over a new leaf. "Yeah, I guess I did," he said. "I know I tried to."

He wasn't lying. When Gino's departure started to become a reality, he seemed to want to get involved with everything around the house—he was happy helping my mother and sisters shop for food, giving my father a hand making pizza, helping me make more free throws, and even baiting his own fish hook with live bloodworms. He had come a long way from those earlier moments of the summer when he would rather veg out in front of the TV, hit the sack early, push food around his plate, or suffer long crying jags alone on the cold bathroom floor.

"Did you make all those changes because you realized you were gonna miss us once you left?" I asked.

Gino sat on the bed and took a breath. "I was definitely afraid to come here," he admitted. "You always seemed comfortable with yourself. You're into sports, you're funny, and you're smart. I've always felt like a pudgy, awkward kid around you. But not toward the end of this summer."

Gino's intelligence and sensitivity for a ten-year old amazed me at times. I felt like he was ready to be fucked with, so I said: "Sounds like you got the hots for me, cuz."

"Oh God, no!" he screamed, and his laugh had never been more genuine.

We walked downstairs, I had Gino walk a glass of Scotch over to my father and we found our seats at the dining room table, along with Aunt Mary, Rosalie, Jack, NuNu, and Frankie. Little Jackie sat in a highchair between his mom and dad. We began bullshitting about this and that when my mother walked out of the kitchen carrying loaves of hot Italian bread and a giant bowl of tuna fish with mayonnaise and chopped hard-boiled eggs. I put up a little protest before I ripped off a piece of bread and begrudgingly dumped a forkful of tuna on my plate. I took a bite and grimaced. My disgust was obvious to Lorraine, who couldn't help but hide a little laugh behind her hand.

"Stop it, A.J.," my mother hissed. "Just eat."

Despite Gino kicking my foot under the chair, I just couldn't keep my mouth shut.

"Am I the only one who's pissed off we're eating tuna fish?" I announced.

My father wasn't much for scolding me, so he didn't say anything after I popped off. But I couldn't help but notice he was deep in thought, taking delicate, little bites of tuna off his fork.

"Lilly, let me ask you a question," he slowly began. "You know my favorite brand, and the only brand I ever want on this table is Bumble Bee, right?"

"Of course," my mother proudly said, almost standing up in indignation when she added. "Why, what are you trying to say?"

The family began to look a bit uncomfortable in their chairs. "I'm saying this ain't Bumble Bee."

"Your ass, it isn't Bumble Bee," my mother hollered. "I know what tuna fish to buy."

Now my father was almost standing up. "Lower your voice," he warned her. "Don't let me go to the garbage can and find something else."

My mother leaned back in her chair very confidently and kept on eating. "You can do whatever the hell you want."

An eerie silence fell upon the room as my father dropped his fork, spit out his food, pushed his plate aside, and walked over to the kitchen garbage.

Rosalie and Lorraine looked white as ghosts. "Ma, are you sure you bought the right tuna?" Rosalie whispered.

"I'm tired of his bullshit," she said. "Let him go shopping if he thinks he can do a better job."

I remember feeling weirdly vindicated over this crappy choice of supper, but that was immediately followed by how worried I was that this damn tuna fish dinner was about to seriously fracture our family. And on Gino's last night, no less.

At this point Gino was shitting a brick and I was bracing myself for the kind of dinner fight I'd seen before—where my father would no doubt flip over the table. We listened to him fishing through the pail before we heard the unmistakable sound of tin cans in his hands. "*StarKist!*" he yelled. "She bought fuckin' StarKist. Was it an accident or out of spite?"

My father kicked the garbage can over and began to march upstairs to their bedroom, despite a constant plea from Rosalie: "Daddy, please, don't do this."

What made this fight so much scarier than the others is that several seconds after he trudged up the steps—which had always been a clear warning for all of us to stay away—my mother followed right behind him. That was a first. And that scared us all.

"Can you believe this?" Lorraine said, as the footsteps and the sound of moving furniture above our heads grew louder. "Now what?"

"Just everybody be quiet," I pleaded, with my stomach in a knot. "If we go up there it's only gonna get worse."

Everyone's appetite was shot, so Gino and I began to walk the dishes into the kitchen to be washed. No sooner had I turned on the hot water, I heard a needle scratch an album on the dining room stereo and the low rumblings of a recording filled the house.

I ran into the dining room to see Rosalie hunched over the hi-fi. "Rosalie, what the hell are you doing?"

Gino was right behind me, "Please, Ro, I'm scared. This can't be a good idea."

A few seconds later, I heard the familiar first few notes of "Cabaret" bouncing off the walls.

What good is sitting all alone in your room . . .

"This is crazy," I said.

"This is Liza!" Gino screamed.

"Ro," I continued. "What are you doing? Daddy's gonna go apeshit!"

Just then we saw my father marching down the stairs wearing eyeliner, white pancake makeup on his face, and bright red lipstick. He was jingling a bunch of loose change in his pocket and was singing à la Joel Grey from the movie.

We'd been had. My father had set it all up, buying the *Cabaret* album and hiding it from us as soon as he got home. He used all the women as accomplices. Just when it couldn't get any crazier, Rosalie and my mother put sequined headbands on Gino and me and, with the help of Lorraine, began to apply the proper Minnelli stage makeup to our faces. Right down to a Sally Bowles sequined beauty mark on her left cheek. Amid shrieks of laughter and mild protests (mainly on my part) we got up and sang most of the whole album with my father and the rest of my family. Not surprisingly, Gino knew almost all the words—from "Cabaret" to "Willkommen" to "Mein Herr."

At one point between songs, Gino grabbed my father's arm. "Uncle Al, when did you get this album?"

"I snuck it home today," he said. "You think I forgot how much you told us you love Liza?"

My mother, who'd done a masterful job in the con, sat at the table smiling at everything going on around her. She grabbed Gino in a hug. "Tell the truth, Gino. Were you scared?"

"Scared shitless!" Gino laughed. "But I'm so happy you pulled it off."

After an hour or so of songs and stories that wrapped up the summer in a nice, tight bundle, we all hugged and kissed good night and made our way to our bedrooms. Gino fell asleep with makeup on and the sequined headband still on his head. I didn't think it right to disturb him.

When Uncle Larry showed up the next morning to take Gino home, he met a new person. Gino wasn't the macho, street-fighting lothario Uncle Larry might have hoped he'd find, but now his boy beamed with a quiet confidence, resolve, and inner freedom. Uncle Larry was touched when he listened to the story of the *Cabaret* shenanigans the night before. He took my father aside and the two shared the warm and knowing embraces only brothers can muster.

My father sent him off with the hard advice he'd been seeking for years.

"You have a wonderful son, Larry. He may not carry on your name, but he's going to carry on your warmth, your sensitivity, your humor, and your love. What more can a father ask?"

Uncle Larry teared up and squeezed my father as he got in his car. "How can I ever thank you, Al?"

"Just love your son as he is, Larry. He's a Benza. He's ours."

EPILOGUE

SHAMBALA

After that sweet summer of 1974, it seemed as though my life had turned into one of those old black-and-white Hollywood films, where stacks of screaming newspaper headlines would roll off a truck and the pages on a wall calendar would fly off and spin wildly at the screen. Confidence-breaking and earth-shattering things were happening at a clip that was too surreal to believe.

I became sexually active at thirteen. I threw myself headlong into basketball, despite butting heads with the legendary coach, Mr. Smith, and found myself cut from the team every year until my junior season. I surrounded myself with a bunch of wild boys who got their kicks breaking into schools, stealing clamming boats, and doing anything the local Mafiosi asked of us.

But it wasn't long before I walked away from college to spend my days and nights to watch my father slowly and undeniably dying. His old pal God wasn't going to stage his exit too hastily. With all the drinking and temper tantrums, you'd think my father would've wrapped himself around a telephone pole or had himself a massive coronary. No. Not my father. God took his time with him. It was a final suffering act that got progressively worse and harder to deal with for eleven long years.

He was dealt an incurable form of cancer called mycosis fungoides. In the terms of a bitter layman and dismayed son, it's basically a disease in which lymphocytes (a type of white blood cell) become malignant and affect the skin. First, patches of the skin start to itch terribly. In due time, the damaged skin magically turns into burn marks and takes on a higher level of pain. Finally, the affected areas turn as brittle as an old rose petal and disintegrate in your hands. After a couple of years and dozens of home remedies (including coating him with extra-virgin olive oil and wrapping him up in Saran wrap), we forced him to take further steps by seeing numerous oncologists, who all meant well but did no more than use my father as a guinea pig for their next big medical paper.

It quickly became apparent that we had to see better doctors in bigger hospitals. I accompanied my father on drives to New York-Presbyterian in Washington Heights or Mount Sinai Hospital in the Bronx, where he would undergo treatments that ranged from ultraviolet A rays directed toward his skin to a cocktail of drugs taken orally as a chaser. In another type of photodynamic therapy, called extracorporeal photo-chemotherapy, my father was fed drugs before some blood cells were taken from his body, put under a special ultraviolet A light, and slammed back into him. Every doctor told him he needed to stay out of the sun for these therapies to have a chance of offering any kind of remission. But as soon as I drove his big silver Cadillac back from the city and into our driveway, he would stumble into the backyard, hop in the pool, and get to work on his garden. He was gonna go out doing things his way.

Finally, when things got really bad, we went to Manhattan's Memorial Sloan Kettering so the big dogs could take a look at him. This, in my opinion, is what expedited his slow, agonizing, and inevitable death.

The docs at Sloan brought out their big radiation guns, which used high-energy X-rays to kill cancer cells or to keep them from growing. When that didn't work, they used internal radiation therapy, in which radioactive substances sealed in needles and wires, and sometimes catheters, were placed directly into or near the cancer. But since mycosis fungoides is a cancer that affects all organs, and our skin is the largest organ, it was futile to even attack his insides, since his outward appearance was starting to resemble that of victims of the new dreaded disease: AIDS.

And thus began my father's years on the "AIDS floors," where all the victims of "the gay cancer" were put up. The sad thing was, whenever we'd take my father for slow, agonizing walks around a hospital's hallways, we would pass rooms and beds and wheelchairs of sick men, much younger than my father, who possessed the same look of impending death. I spent more time with grieving gay men in hospital hallways during my teenage years than I did with all the pretty girls in high school.

In the last summer of my father's life, Uncle Larry got in touch with a Swiss doctor who got his hands on a "wonder drug" not yet approved by the FDA that was supposed to restore my father's skin and other organs, getting him at last to a peaceful remission and on his feet again. The man's name was Dr. Willie Kreist (ironically pronounced *Christ*). Hardly where the help would come from, considering my father's staunch atheism. Unfortunately, the drug wasn't covered by any insurance company, and the price per injection was through the roof, especially since it would be one injection every day for God knows how long. Uncle Larry footed the bill for months without so much as blinking one of his gorgeous green eyes, until the day my father's adhesions healed and the holes behind his knees magically filled up. Though the hair on his head never came back, his trademark mustache grew back thick as ever. He was able to sit up and walk on his own. Before long he was dancing in his hospital room with his big, black nurse Roberta while she sang, "What's Love Got to Do with It?" We were over the moon.

Now he could go to the beach with his grandchildren. He could clam again with the family.

He would sit on the porch with my mother, the two of them rolling out his hospital bills like a scroll and laughing like hounds. "They could build a fuckin' casino with this money," he said.

But the wonder drug lasted only so long.

I'll spare you the rest of the gory details. Before my father entered his final resting place, North Shore University Hospital in Manhasset, he was administered various kinds of oral, injected, and topical chemotherapies. The most debilitating by far was the nitrogen mustard. It turned his skin so dark, he made Gandhi look like a white boy.

In the winter of 1985, after seven months of watching him fade away in a sea of blue and white sheets, we sent all the doctors away and I became more like a sentry than a son. Enough with the needles; enough with the tests; enough with the scans. Put the morphine drip on high and let the man go.

And that's what we did.

He was gone in March. My wonderful, sweet mother died on Christmas morning five years later.

"Don't worry about me," she'd told me one morning, lying in her hospice bed. "I had a wonderful life. All my children lived next to me, and my grandchildren come through my kitchen door every morning before school. I had it all. Now . . . I just miss your father too, too much."

What do you say to that?

In the ten years that followed, I married and divorced my high school sweetheart before selling my house and moving to Greenwich Village to work as a gossip columnist for the *New York Daily News*. Gino and I kept in touch as much as we could once we found we could practically throw rocks at each other from our Greenwich Village apartments—mine on Horatio Street, his on West Tenth Street. But, because we were busy making names for ourselves in the big city, we never did spend that much extended time with each other. By this time, my little cousin was busy getting his master's degree in social work from NYU and began working as a psychotherapist. Whenever we did find time to grab drinks at the local watering holes, we would talk about our dating nightmares and the fact that we couldn't believe we were both lucky enough to be doing the things we loved the most. Those get-togethers lasted well into the 1990s before Gino settled down with a great guy and I was off to Los Angeles to work in TV. With both our lives at warp speed, it seemed we were unfortunately headed toward rarely seeing each other except for at weddings and funerals. But whenever those occasions came about, we picked up our conversations as if not a single day had passed. And we always cherished the times when we effortlessly managed to bring up the minutia of that one summer long ago. We still laughed about my mother's feeble attempt at tacos. We shuddered at the mere mention of wooden dolls with busted teeth. We reminisced about that magic fishing hole. And we both couldn't forget the color of Julia Thorne's haunting, pale blue eyes.

I know Gino was genuinely happy for me and my good fortune at chasing down all my dreams. But I'm not sure I was able to properly convey just how proud I was watching his career take off in a direction that seems so obvious in hindsight. The fact that he was able to go on and help people whose sense of self and prior life experience had blocked their ability to heal and get what they wanted out of life gave me chills. And the simplistic beauty that his main purpose every day was to help people feel more comfortable in their own skin. Of course that's what he would go on and do!

When Gino's brother, Larry, succumbed to AIDS in 1998, I flew in for the funeral. I can't say I was shocked at all to see Gino being emotionally tended to by a handsome man with an obvious caring nature. But I was a little surprised to see, in the midst of the huddle of human sorrow, my grieving uncle Larry.

I approached the three of them quietly and put my hand on Uncle Larry's frail shoulder. He turned to me and the waterworks started. It was like we were beneath the peach tree all over again.

"Oh, A.J.," he sobbed. "Larry's at peace. My son is finally at peace now." And then, extending his arms to Gino and his male friend, he said to me, "This is Gino's wonderful partner, Glen. Glen, this is my brother's son."

"Your dad was Uncle Al, am I right?" Glen said, giving me a warm hug and a long handshake.

"I take it Gino told you a few stories," I said.

And then Gino burst out, hugging me. "I told him *every* story. *Everything* we ever did."

And there we were, the four of us, almost a quarter century removed from the dire phone call Uncle Larry had made to my home that fateful night. What seemed almost impossible to accept that very night was, at this moment, wonderful and sweet and real.

The next time I saw Gino was two years later, at Uncle Larry's funeral, after his consecutive bouts with lung and brain cancer: another Benza boy making a loud exit. This time around Gino and Glen were wearing commitment rings. They told me of their plans to one day make it legal, "if that ever becomes possible."

"How was it for your pops in the end?" I asked.

"Ugh," Gino sighed. "He came out of his coma at the very end long enough to tell me how thrilled he was for my happiness. How fond he was of Glen."

"That's the best you could ask for, I suppose," I said, genuinely satisfied for my little cousin. And then there was a long, awkward pause.

"I hope I'm not imagining this," Gino told me. "But I think his last words to me were, 'I have such a handsome and happy son.'"

"He was probably loaded," I joked.

Then, amid the bouts of tears and bursts of laughter that accompany all Italian funerals, Gino and I recalled stories of that glorious summer of 1974.

"The best summer," he said, his words breezing past us and softly landing somewhere among the big sprays of mums surrounding his father's casket.

He was speaking to his father in the moment when he said, "The best summer of my life."

And I was speaking to mine when I said, "The best summer of *our lives.*"

ACKNOWLEDGMENTS

There is no book if it were not for the memories and antics of my beautiful sisters Rosalie and Lorraine, my brothers-in-law Jack and Frankie, and *brothers* Jack and Joe; my cousins Arlene Benza, Richard Mantia, Grace Marie Haggerty, Phil Mattera, and most of all my cousin Gino Benza; thanks to the recollections from lifelong friends Joe Colucci, Ramsey Dabby, Pauline Meyer, and Debbie Rossitto. Thank you all for putting such vivid color to that summer of '74.

I owe a lot (much more than his fee) to my agent Steve Troha and to Ruth Pomerance at Folio Lit. And to my great team at Simon & Schuster: Mitchell Ivers, Jen Bergstrom, Louise Burke, Natasha Simons, Felice Javit, and Trish Boczkowski—wherever you've disappeared to! To my supportive

ACKNOWLEDGMENTS

friends Ro Terenzio, Neal Gumpel, "Uncle" Kevin Dornan, and Adam Tenenbaum, who bought me the laptop so I could begin this book. A kiss on the ring to Harvey Weinstein because whenever I've called, he's always been there—no questions asked.

A big hug to Richie Folk, for being a good son and a great big brother.

To my wonderful uncle Larry and my unbelievable mother and father, Al and Lily Benza. They were just too good to be true.

And, finally, to the newest Benzas—my Roxy and my Rocco. Daddy loves you with all his heart, his soul and his guts! Should either of you grow up to be an author, write nice things about me.